HANNAH ROARS

—AND BIRTHS A NEW BREED—

Greg Buzzanco

Hannah Roars: And Births a New Breed
Copyright 2015 by Greg Buzzanco
Published by Triumphant Life Church

All rights reserved. No part of this book may be reproduced, stored in a retrieval system, or transmitted in any form or by any means-electronic, mechanical, photocopy, recording, or otherwise-without prior written permission of the copyright owner.

Scripture quotations marked KJV are taken from the King James Version of the Bible. Public domain.

Scripture quotations marked AMP are taken from the Amplified® Bible, copyright © 1954, 1958, 1962, 1964, 1965, 1987 by The Lockman Foundation. Used by permission.

Scripture quotations marked YLT are taken from Young's Literal Translation, 1898. Public domain.

Bracketed insertions in Scripture quotations are the author's own.

ISBN: 978-1-943662-00-5

Contents

Chapter 1: A Prophetic Picture of Things to Come   7
   About the Title: What Do You Mean, *Hannah Roars*?
   Prophetic Prayer and Prophecy
   Sacred Cow Tipping: Trials Alone Will Not Perfect You
   More Sacred Cow Tipping
   Types, Shadows, and Examples vs. Reality and Substance
   Trends vs. Truth: Observing the Law vs. Fulfilling the Law
   Cleansing the Temple
   Out with the Old and In with the New
   The Litmus Test of the Prophetic Ministry

Chapter 2: A Strong Foundation   21
   Prayer and Sports
   Transitioning
   The Suddenlies
   The Anointed Spoken Word
   The Rock Out of the Mountain
   It's Time to Push
   A Better Covenant with Better Promises
   A New Level of Grace
   Going Higher
   Full Speed Ahead
   Swift Advancement of God's Kingdom
   Is This Your Vision for the Last Days?

Chapter 3: The Story of Hannah   35
   Darkness Abounds, but Can Not Prevail
   The Time Has Finally Come: Watchmen, Take Your Place!
   The High Calling: The Birthing of the Man-child

Unprecedented Change Is Coming
Hannah and Her Seed
Hannah Means "Grace"
God Meant It for Good
The Game Changers Are Being Released
One Day Is as a Thousand Years
The Temple Will Be Completed
It's Time to Pray for Rain

Chapter 4: The Feast of Tabernacles   47
Beyond First Fruits
The Corn, the Wine, and the Oil
From Pentecost to Tabernacles
Did Joel Flunk Meteorology Class?
If…
The Lord's Prayer: More Than a Religious Exercise
Ready or Not, Here I Come!
Original Intent
The God of Armies
Shiloh: The Place of Rest
Aggressive Prayer
The Zeal of the Lord
A Changing of the Guard
Approved Building Materials
No More Canaanites in God's House
Double for Your Trouble
Come Up Higher
Rousing the Roar
Take Your Rightful Place

Chapter 5: Hannah Roars   67
Time to Roar
Passion and Persistence
The Name of Jesus
Importunity: The Quality of Being Shameless and Offensively Bold
Give Me Three Loaves
The Anointed Spoken Word

Shamelessly Bold
The Lord Is Coming Out!
Avenge Me of My Adversary

Chapter 6: The Roar of the Lord   83
Great Focus
Roaring Fires
Messengers of Fire
The Two Witnesses
Tremendous Power through Energized Prayer
Mockery and False Judgment Silenced
Groaning and Travailing
God Has Not Given Us a Spirit of Timidity
Shalom
The High Calling

Chapter 7: Hannah's Prophecy   99
Unprecedented Trouble
That I Might Know Him
Revelation 12: This Is a "Daddy's Boy"
Hannah Prophesies the Overturning of All Things
"Overturn" Times Three
The Noise of Many Waters

Chapter 8: Roaring Rivers   109
The Pouring Out of the Water
The Spotless Bride
The Pearly Gates
The Temple
Where Did the Temple Go?
No More Curse
Go Ahead, Jump!

Chapter 9: Roaring 101   119
The ABCs of How to Roar
Praying Divine Mysteries
Standing on the Shoulders of Giants
Divine Intervention

Lord of the Breakthrough
Let's Go Deeper
Who Will Rise Up?
Resolution Precedes Revolution

Appendix **129**
General Scriptures on the Power of Prayer
Scriptural Things to Pray For
Prophetic Prayers and Decrees for This Hour

Chapter 1: A Prophetic Picture of Things to Come

Chapter 1

A Prophetic Picture of Things to Come

About the Title: What Do You Mean, *Hannah Roars*?

I had been noticing an unprecedented level of focus, intensity, and travail at our leadership prayer meetings for quite some time. I had been in many fervent prayer meetings over the decades, but I knew this was not business as usual. So I asked the Lord what was going on, and He spoke the word *Hannah* to me and revealed that great, unparalleled change was coming to the earth.

The story of Hannah in the Bible has intrigued me since childhood. As I studied this amazing story, I had no idea what I was about to discover. I did a bit of digging into the original Hebrew and discovered the Hebraic text actually reads that "Hannah roared!" I will take a deeper look at this in Chapter 5.

Most English translations do not show this meaning. It is clearly revealed by reading this verse in the original Old Testament Hebrew, but first, let's look at it in the King James Version.

> **But unto Hannah he** [Hannah's husband] **gave a worthy portion; for he loved Hannah: but the Lord shut up her womb. And her adversary also provoked her sore, for to make her fret, because the Lord had shut up her womb (1 Samuel 1:5-6).**

Young's Literal translation does not say "adversary"; it reads "adversity." Here it is in Young's Literal Translation.

HANNAH ROARS

And to Hannah he giveth a certain portion—double, for he hath loved Hannah, and Jehovah hath shut her womb; and her adversity hath also provoked her greatly, so as to make her tremble, for Jehovah hath shut up her womb (1 Samuel 1:5-6 YLT).

The word *tremble* (as Young's Literal Translation translates it) is the Hebrew word *ra'am*.[1] The King James Version translated this word as "fret," but this Hebrew word *ra'am* actually means "to thunder" or "to roar"! This Hebrew word is used thirteen times in the Old Testament and this is the only time it is translated as *fret*; most of the other times it is translated as "thunder" or "roar."

Hannah wasn't trembling or fretting because of her adversity; she was thundering and roaring. Here is what verse 6 is actually stating: Hannah's adversity, her trouble, her distress, and her affliction provoked her to anger, which made her thunder or roar! She entered into a place of aggressive, covenantal prayer that would shake heaven and earth.

That *roar* would take her from a state of barrenness to a state of remarkable fruitfulness. Many other women in that day were barren and prayed for God to intervene but there was no change. Hannah did more than pray; Hannah *roared* and brought forth a man-child who would completely change the nation of Israel and indeed the world. Few have ever been willing and determined to seek out and discover the spiritual law of life and productivity that Hannah tapped into. However, I believe that God is raising up a people in this hour who will follow in Hannah's footsteps and be used to birth a new thing that will change everything.

Prophetic Prayer and Prophecy

The story of Hannah and her inspired prayer and prophecy are more relevant today than at any other time in history. Today, through His bride, the Holy Spirit inspires prayers and decrees that are birthing the fulfillment of Hannah's prayer and prophecy. You have probably heard of Hannah's prayer, but did you ever hear of her prophecy? Yes, Hannah prophesied. In fact, her prophecy is one of the most powerful,

---

1. James Strong, *Strong's Exhaustive Concordance* (Peabody, MA: Hendrickson Publishers, 2007), H7481.

A Prophetic Picture of Things to Come

earth-shattering and transforming prophecies ever uttered by the lips of a human.

Hannah experienced amazing personal breakthrough. She learned how to turn adversity and what seemed like impossible circumstances into triumphs and victories. Hannah's breakthrough was a type and shadow. It is an example foreshadowing the new thing God is doing in the earth today. This includes the unprecedented breakthrough that God has in store for His people. I don't believe you are reading this by chance. God's hand is upon you to be a part of the unparalleled release of His glory and the advancement of His kingdom that is greater than the earth has ever seen. It is possible that you have experienced what may seem to be more than your share of difficulties and hardships in life, but remember the principle that the greater the struggle a butterfly has breaking out of its cocoon, the greater its wingspan will be; thus, the greater its ability to fly. I believe an unequaled level of grace is coming to the people of God that will empower them to go from barrenness to fruitfulness. Like Hannah, many in the body of Christ are about to learn how to turn extraordinary adversity into unprecedented triumph. God is about to turn our mourning into dancing. It may not appear like it right now, but it's time for God's people to rejoice and sing! Everything is about to dramatically change.

> **Sing, O barren, thou that didst not bear; break forth into singing, and cry aloud, thou that didst not travail with child: for more are the children of the desolate than the children of the married wife, saith the Lord (Isaiah 54:1).**

Before we find out how Hannah learned to roar and how we can too, allow me to lay some groundwork.

Sacred Cow Tipping: Trials Alone Will Not Perfect You

Many Christians falsely believe that trials and adversities automatically perfect believers and bring them to maturity. If this were the case, then most believers would be perfect or at least be on their way to perfection and spiritual maturity, because no one is exempt from adversity. All Christians have had plenty of trials and adversities. It's not the trials alone that perfect us or cause spiritual growth; it's learning how to overcome, conquer, and rise above adversity through the victory that Christ has already purchased at the cross and through the authority that He has consequently given us. We must learn to use adversity to our advantage and make the most of unfavorable situations. God does not want us to be dominated by circumstances but to overcome them. We are called to walk by faith and not by sight. We can learn by looking at how Jesus responded when He was tested and tried in the wilderness: He spoke the Word of God from His heart straight in the face of the enemy and his lies.

One practical thing that you can do to make sure you are not letting hardships go to waste is to speak forth the truth of God's Word, even in the face of adverse circumstances that seem to make it appear that God's Word isn't true. You probably won't feel like speaking God's Word in the midst of a test, but you must. Don't give in to the temptation to grumble, complain, and look at the circumstances. In every test or trial you should ask, "What does God's Word have to say about this situation?" Find out what God's Word has to say about your situation and focus on that. Fill your mouth with His Word. Here are some Scriptures that should be planted deep within our hearts and on our lips in the midst of every trial.

> **These things I have spoken unto you, that in me ye might have peace. In the world ye shall have tribulation: but be of good cheer; I have overcome the world (John 16:33).**
>
> **Ye are of God, little children, and have overcome them: because greater is he that is in you, than he that is in the world (1 John 4:4).**
>
> **And they overcame him by the blood of the Lamb, and by the word of their testimony; and they loved not their lives unto the death (Revelation 12:11).**
>
> **For whatsoever is born of God overcometh the world: and this is the victory that overcometh the world, even our faith (1 John 5:4).**

God's Word clearly states that He wants His children to develop to the level of being able to change their circumstances instead of being

A Prophetic Picture of Things to Come

dominated by them. The Bible is full of examples of people who took the Word of God and the promises of God and turned hopeless situations around.

More Sacred Cow Tipping

Many believe that God is in charge of everything in this earth or at least in their personal lives. We must never forget that God delegates. He says in Psalm 115:16 that the heavens are His, but the earth He has given unto man. He has delegated authority on the earth to mankind from the beginning and continues to do so. The fact that man has misused this authority and has made significantly poor choices has not stopped God from delegating. In Matthew 28, Jesus states that all authority in heaven and on earth has been given to Him; but He does not stop there! He goes on to state that we are to go forth in His name and disciple nations. He has clearly delegated to the church, which is His body, the authority that He had just received from the Father after His resurrection! I am well aware that many teachers in the church are telling people that we are quite limited in what we can change in our lives and in the earth because they think God is sovereign and in complete control. However, an in-depth study of the Scriptures will clearly reveal that God, in His sovereignty, can indeed do whatever He chooses; and He has chosen to delegate His authority on the earth to His church, His body! Even though the church has neglected her authoritative position or has not always used that authority wisely, we must remember that the Scripture states in Romans 11:29 that the gifts and callings of God are without repentance.

Many Christians are not effectively using the authority they have been given to bring significant change to their lives or to the world around them. They have often settled for anything that comes across their paths, thinking that God must have some mysterious reason for allowing their situation. Thank God Hannah was not of that mindset. She did not settle for anything but God's best and ended up giving God her best. We need to have a biblical worldview and not just a religious one. The Bible is replete with passages and examples of how we are not to be ruled by circumstances but indeed are to rule over them.

HANNAH ROARS

Every sincere disciple of Christ should know and live by the following verse:

For if by one man's offence death reigned by one; much more they which receive abundance of grace and of the gift of righteousness shall reign in life by one, Jesus Christ (Romans 5:17).

Did you catch that? We are to reign in life and that includes now, not just in the sweet by and by. Hannah didn't settle for barrenness with the mindset of, *I might be barren, unfulfilled, and living way below my covenantal rights and privileges as a daughter of Abraham, but someday, when I get to heaven, I will really have it made.* No, she pressed in and learned the secret of bringing heaven to earth. We are living in the hour when many will learn to do the same. God's will is about to be done on earth as it is in heaven. These are days of unprecedented change, but we must learn how to release the *roar* like Hannah did. Before we can get into the specifics and the how-to of releasing the *roar*, I have to lay some more foundation.

Types, Shadows, and Examples vs. Reality and Substance

First Corinthians 10:11 tells us that everything that was written concerning God's people in the Old Testament was actually written for today's New Testament believers. For example, in the Old Testament, when God's people celebrated the Feast of Passover, they were just observing the type and shadow of the Lamb of God who was going to come from heaven and be slain and take away the sin of the world. In the Old Testament, we read that during Passover they placed the blood of a lamb over the lintels and doorposts of their homes. Today, in the New Testament (New Covenant), Jesus' blood is placed over the lintels and doorposts of the hearts of those who put their faith in Jesus as the sacrifice and payment for their sins. Jesus' blood, that washes us as Christians and is continually applied over our lives and homes, is a fulfillment of the type and shadow of the Old Testament observance of the Feast of Passover. We don't need to sacrifice and consume a lamb every spring at the time of Passover. We need to receive Jesus, who is our Passover Lamb, once and for all as our Lord and Savior.

A Prophetic Picture of Things to Come

Purge out therefore the old leaven, that ye may be a new lump, as ye are unleavened. For even Christ our passover is sacrificed for us (1 Corinthians 5:7).

Trends vs. Truth: Observing the Law vs. Fulfilling the Law

Some Christians today are being told they need to observe the Old Testament laws, feasts, and holy days. I know this is a very controversial topic, but the Bible is clear: Jesus did not come to observe the Law but to *fulfill* the Law. There is a big difference between observing the Law (which is just keeping a natural type and shadow) and fulfilling the Law (which is experiencing the spiritual fulfillment, completion, and accomplishment of what the Law pointed to).

Let no man therefore judge you in meat, or in drink, or in respect of an holyday, or of the new moon, or of the sabbath days: which are a shadow [example] of things to come; but the body is of Christ (Colossians 2:16-17).

Hannah's story is a type and foreshadowing of a group of people who, like Hannah, are dissatisfied with walking below their covenantal privileges and who will be aggressive enough in their spirits to press into the Lord and do something about it.

And from the days of John the Baptist until now the kingdom of heaven suffereth violence, and the violent take it by force (Matthew 11:12).

You can learn to release the roar, like Hannah, or you can remain in a state of barrenness and fall short of the call and plan of God for your life.

God is raising up a people who will aggressively respond to His high calling and will not settle for fruitlessness, spiritual barrenness, or the status quo. God requires a people who are not content with a compromised, powerless Christian life. The church is to be the light of the world, a city set on a hill that cannot be hid. Unfortunately, much of the light within us has been hid under the bushel of the flesh and the soul. The Great Commission, defined in Matthew 28 and Mark 16, instructs the church to teach, train, and disciple the nations of the world while displaying great power and authority. Instead, we have seen the world influencing the church to become more like it is. We have seen the church remain relatively complacent and silent as it witnessed the world's attempts at eradicating God and Christianity from schools and governments. Don't be dismayed! Great change is coming to the church and to the earth. God is raising up Christians who will be His instruments of change. They will not acquiesce to the world's standards or methodologies.

Cleansing the Temple

> **Love not the world, neither the things that are in the world. If any man love the world, the love of the Father is not in him (1 John 2:15).**

The methods and ways of the world have permeated much of the church today. Madison Avenue marketing techniques are routinely employed in church growth seminars. The Bible makes it repeatedly clear that we are not to go down to Egypt (a type of the world) for help. If you look at many ministries today, they differ very little from secular corporations.

> **Woe to them that go down to Egypt for help; and stay on horses, and trust in chariots, because they are many; and in horsemen, because they are very strong; but they look not unto the Holy One of Israel, neither seek the Lord! (Isaiah 31:1).**

> **Thus saith the Lord; Cursed be the man that trusteth in man, and maketh flesh his arm, and whose heart departeth from the Lord (Jeremiah 17:5).**

I would encourage you to stop right now and ask God to reveal any love of the world or trust in the world's methods that is in you and confess it before Him. God will cleanse you right now. You can be changed right now. First John 1:9 tells us that if we confess our sins before Him, He will not only forgive us but will cleanse us from them. It is a lie from hell that says that believers can't be free from all manner

A Prophetic Picture of Things to Come

of sin and worldliness. Romans 6 tells us that we have already been set free from the power of sin by Jesus, and that we are no longer slaves of sin, but slaves of righteousness.

> **Being then made free from sin, ye became the servants of righteousness (Romans 6:18).**

> **For the law of the Spirit of life in Christ Jesus hath made me free from the law of sin and death (Romans 8:2).**

Put God's Word in your heart and in your mouth. The Word will become a manifest reality to those who do. True transformation comes by the renewing of our minds with the Word of God. Christians are called to fight the good fight of faith. Believing God's Word in the face of the lies of the enemy is not always easy. The attack, even from the beginning in the garden, has always been to get us to doubt God's Word. According to the Scriptures, the enemy has already been defeated. We don't have to defeat him. We do, however, have to *enforce* his defeat by using the Sword of the Spirit, which is the Word of God. Jesus used the Scriptures declaring *it is written* when dealing with the enemy. Meditate on and declare the following Scriptures from your heart when dealing with the enemy.

> **Who** [God] **hath delivered us from the power of darkness, and hath translated us into the kingdom of his dear Son: in whom we have redemption through his blood, even the forgiveness of sins (Colossians 1:13-14).**

> **And** [Jesus] **having spoiled** [defeated] **principalities and powers, he made a shew of them openly, triumphing over them in it** [Jesus' life, death, and resurrection] **(Colossians 2:15).**

Out with the Old and In with the New

The ministry of Eli and his sons (the religious leaders of Hannah's day) was a ministry full of lethargy, compromise, and corruption, but all of that was going to change because of what Hannah was about to birth. Things would never be the same because Hannah gave birth to Samuel. There is a birthing of a new breed of Christians in the earth today. A passion similar to Hannah's is rising up within the church, and like Hannah, nothing is going to stop this passion. Are you content with seeing the world and ungodly people in places of authority over the people of God? Are you content with seeing dead religion flourish while true believers around the world are being mocked and persecuted? Jesus said that Christians would suffer persecution, but He also promised deliverance to those who would aggressively and insistently ask for change.

And shall not God avenge his own elect, which cry day and night unto Him, though he bear long with them? (Luke 18:7).

Many of God's people are no longer content with Saul (ungodly leadership) being on the throne while David (God's anointed) remains hidden in the caves of Adullam (see 1 Samuel 22:1). Saul's reign as king was plagued with a behavioral pattern of partial obedience and a tendency to want to please the people rather than obey God (see 1 Samuel 15:1-23). David made some obvious mistakes but had a heart to obey God fully. The Bible itself testifies to this fact in Acts 13:22:

"And when he [God] had removed him [Saul], he raised up unto them David to be their king; to whom also he gave their testimony, and said, I have found David the son of Jesse, a man after mine own heart, which shall fulfill all my will."

There is something beginning to rise up in a people with the heart of David—a cry for the freedom and deliverance of God's people and for His entire creation to be released from the bondages of sin, oppression, and corruption. This has to do with the spiritual fulfillment of Hannah's story. The *roar* has begun.

Let the priests, the ministers of the Lord, weep between the porch and the altar, and let them say, Spare thy people, O Lord, and give not thine heritage to reproach, that the heathen should rule over them: wherefore should they say among the people, Where is their God? (Joel 2:17).

A Prophetic Picture of Things to Come

The Litmus Test of the Prophetic Ministry

A powerful, prophetic anointing rested upon Hannah. She also had a strong prayer anointing. It's interesting how so many people today claim to be prophets or claim to have a prophetic anointing but have no vital prayer life. The Bible is clear that true prophets are intercessors.

But if they be prophets, and if the word of the Lord be with them, let them now make intercession to the Lord of hosts (Jeremiah 27:18).

Did you see that? Read it again carefully. Jeremiah 27:18 states that if someone is a true prophet, he or she will also be one who will make intercession for the people.

Chapter 2: A Strong Foundation

Chapter 2
A Strong Foundation

Prayer and Sports

There are many types of prayer, but the prayer of intercession involves praying for others. Praying for yourself is a valid way to pray, but it is not intercession. You cannot intercede for yourself. Intercession, by definition, involves praying for others. When you are praying for others, you are interceding for them.

The *Oxford Dictionary* defines intercession as "the action of intervening on behalf of another, or the action of praying on behalf of another person."[2]

The Bible shows us that there are many different kinds of prayer. We can see this from the following Scripture:

Praying always with all prayer and supplication in the Spirit, and watching thereunto with all perseverance and supplication for all saints (Ephesians 6:18).

This could be better interpreted as *praying with all manner of prayer* or being led by the Spirit. I cannot emphasize enough the importance of looking to and following the leading of the Holy Spirit in times of prayer. Let Him direct your prayer time. Don't enter into prayer with preconceived ideas of how you will pray. He may want you to spend time praying in the Spirit. He may lead you into praise or worship. He may lead you into a time of praying the Word or speaking prophetic

---

2. A.J. Augarde, *The Oxford Dictionary* (Oxford, UK: Oxford University Press, 1981), s.v. "Intercession."

HANNAH ROARS

decrees (inspired utterances of declarations of the will of God). God may lead you into a time of prayer for your life or ministry or He may lead you to pray for others. Much will be accomplished for His glory as we learn to follow the leading of the Holy Spirit. I find praying is similar to surfing. We must learn to catch the wave of the Spirit and stay on the wave until it lands on the shore. Much power will be released and much will be accomplished as we do this.

As Ephesians 6 states, there are many types of prayer. There is the prayer of faith, the prayer of praise and thanksgiving, the prayer of supplication, the prayer of intercession, the prayer of dedication and consecration, to name a few. They are all prayer, or communication with God, but they're different types of prayer with different rules, or spiritual laws, applying to each one. We shouldn't only pray for comfort. We should also pray to get results. Religious people who don't really know God or His Word usually pray comfort prayers. I believe in praying to get results. I believe every scriptural prayer that we pray should be answered and that the answer should be yes. Just make sure you are praying the will of God, which is the Word of God. Make sure you have Scriptures that back up your request. Dead religion and the traditions of men say that God always answers prayers, but that sometimes the answer is *no* or *wait*. You won't find any Scripture for this. Jesus said:

> **And all things, whatsoever ye shall ask in prayer, believing, ye shall receive (Matthew 21:22).**

> **Hitherto have ye asked nothing in my name: ask, and ye shall receive, that your joy may be full (John 16:24).**

Just as there are many different kinds of sports and different rules apply to each sport, so it is with the many different kinds of prayer. Imagine the confusion if you applied the rules of football to the game of basketball. You would have much chaos and confusion. So it is with prayer.

The prayer of faith never uses the words *if it be thy will*. According to Mark 11:24, the prayer of faith believes it receives the desired request right at the time of prayer, even if the answer can't physically be seen with one's natural eyes. The prayer of faith always ends with the glad

A Strong Foundation

tidings, *I believe. I receive. It is mine. I have it now*. Jesus never once used the phrase *if it be thy will* when ministering healing or deliverance to people, and neither should we. We should know what the Bible has to say concerning our inheritance in Christ. Our beliefs and consequent prayers and confessions must be based on God's Word, not on what we observe or experience in the physical realm. All Scripture is given by inspiration of God and is profitable for doctrine, for reproof, for correction, for instruction in righteousness (see 2 Timothy 3:16). Our beliefs and doctrine should come from the Scriptures, not from our experience. Let's bring our experiences up to the level of God's Word and not lower the standard of God's Word down to our experiences. We should know, boldly claim, and appropriate the promises of God that are in His Word. Faith begins where the will of God is known, and His Word is His will. Put God's Word first in your life. Get into the Word and find out what belongs to you. As you do this, faith will come; and just a little faith, according to the lips of Jesus, can move mountains. Your circumstances can and will change as God's Word is activated in your life! A requirement to a successful prayer life is to know His Word, believe His Word, and pray His Word.

> **If ye abide in me, *and my words abide in you*, ye shall ask what ye will, and it shall be done unto you (John 15:7,** emphasis mine**).**
>
> **And this is the confidence that we have in him, that, if we ask any thing according to his will, he heareth us: and if we know that he hear us, whatsoever we ask, we know that we have the petitions that we desired of him (1 John 5:14-15).**
>
> **For all the promises of God in him are yea, and in him Amen, unto the glory of God by us (2 Corinthians 1:20).**

Transitioning

Deuteronomy 28 tells us that barrenness is a curse and fruitfulness is a blessing. Hannah, as a child of God, refused to settle for barrenness. She refused to walk under the curse of the Law. Through faith, she knew that God could remove her barrenness and take away her reproach.

HANNAH ROARS

She prayed to that effect and got her miracle. The church is about to walk in the miraculous as a way of life. The Scripture is about to be fulfilled. Signs and wonders will follow those who believe (see Mark 16:17). It's now time for the greater works of Jesus mentioned in John 14:12.

The Suddenlies

Like Hannah, God is calling us to birth something new in the earth. We are in the time of the *suddenlies*. It's the time for swift, sudden, and violent advancement of the kingdom of God, not a natural violence but a violence or forcefulness in the spirit.

> **And from the days of John the Baptist until now the kingdom of heaven suffereth violence, and the violent take it by force (Matthew 11:12).**

This is not a time to take up natural weapons but spiritual ones.

> **For the weapons of our warfare are not carnal, but mighty through God to the pulling down of strongholds (2 Corinthians 10:4).**

We will be like the Lord, in that His Word will continually be in our mouths.

> **And he had in his right hand seven stars: and out of his mouth went a sharp twoedged sword (Revelation 1:16).**

> **And out of his mouth goeth a sharp sword, that with it he should smite the nations: and he shall rule them with a rod of iron (Revelation 19:15).**

> **And take the helmet of salvation, and the sword of the Spirit, which is the word of God (Ephesians 6:17).**

> **For the word of God is quick [living], and powerful, and sharper than any twoedged sword (Hebrews 4:12).**

A Strong Foundation

Don't skim over these Scriptures casually. They are the words of God. Read them carefully and intently. Let them get down into your spirit and deep into your inner man. That's when the Word of God will begin to work for you.

The first chapter of the book of John tells us that Jesus is the Word of God made flesh. The book of Revelation confirms this.

And he was clothed with a vesture dipped in blood: and his name is called The Word of God (Revelation 19:13).

The Anointed Spoken Word

The most powerful weapon that is, or will ever be, is about to be released in the earth through a people who are completely in love, submission, and unity with the Lord Jesus Christ. That weapon is the anointed, spoken word! The same power that spoke the world into existence is about to be released again. God has truly saved the best wine for last. Look at what God has to say about His Word.

Is not my word like as a fire? saith the Lord; and like a hammer that breaketh the rock in pieces? (Jeremiah 23:29)

Countless times, I've seen God's Word, like a fire, burn out sickness, disease, sin, rebellion, confusion, and oppression from people. Let God's Word go deep within you. His Word will not fail. But you must put God's Word first and keep it in the midst of your heart and on your tongue. You must put the Word to work. You must *employ* the Word, so to speak.

Don't look at the circumstances; look to the Word. Ask yourself, *What does the Word say about my situation?* Hannah looked beyond the circumstance of her barrenness to the promise of God's Word that states that He would remove barrenness from His people (see Exodus 23:26 and Deuteronomy 7:14).

The Rock Out of the Mountain

Hannah would be used to birth great change in the earth and would eventually go on to prophesy the overturn of all the world's kingdoms. I am not talking about modern day *dominionism*, a doctrine which is rooted in greed, ambition, and worldliness, which simply aspires to take over the world's kingdoms. I am speaking of the complete destruction of this world's systems and kingdoms and the rising up of that which is completely different in nature and structure and is infinitely superior—the kingdom of God. This is exactly what is portrayed in Daniel 2. Here we read of a *rock* that is cut out of a mountain without human hands that brings down the world's kingdoms and becomes a great mountain (the kingdom of God) that fills the earth.

God's anointed spoken word is, in fact, a key component to the effectiveness of the rock cut out of the mountain mentioned in Daniel 2. This rock will destroy and break in pieces the ungodly world kingdoms in the last days. The release of the anointed spoken word is the mechanism that will allow us to witness Revelation 11:15: *"the kingdoms of this world are become the kingdoms of our Lord, and of his Christ"* (His Anointed). More on this later.

It's Time to Push

Hannah overcame adversity and birthed a man-child who would change and transform all of Israel and indeed the world. We are about to be used to do the same.

We must be a people of faith and intercession to see God's purposes birthed in the earth. To be a people of faith, we must be a people of the Word. To be a people of intercession, we must be a people of great love. Love for God must be first. This will entail a deep longing to see His desires that are foretold in His Word come to pass on the earth. If we truly love Jesus who is the Head of the body, we will also love His people, His church, which is His body. God is placing His burden on His people and His desire to see them be the glorious church they are called and destined to be.

If we are truly walking with the Lord, we will certainly sense the leading of His Spirit to pray and intercede for His beloved bride, His church. If you love one another, you will certainly take the time to pray for one another. Effective prayer brings great change. James 5:16 states, *"the effectual fervent prayer of a righteous man availeth much."* The

A Strong Foundation

Amplified Bible states, *"the earnest (heartfelt, continued) prayer of a righteous man makes tremendous power available."* Prayer is joining forces with God to see His will accomplished in our lives and in the earth. Let's release that tremendous power to see the great changes spoken of in His Word for this hour come to pass in the earth.

Isaiah 62 says that we are not to give God any rest until He makes His people a praise in the earth. This verse exemplifies the spirit of prayer and intercession that is coming upon those who love the Lord and are called according to His purpose.

> **I have set watchmen upon thy walls, O Jerusalem, which shall never hold their peace day nor night: ye that make mention of the Lord, keep not silence, and give him no rest, till he establish, and till he make Jerusalem a praise in the earth (Isaiah 62:6-7).**

Hebrews 12 tells us that Jerusalem is actually a *type* or *foreshadow* of the church.

> **But ye are come unto mount Sion, and unto the city of the living God, the heavenly Jerusalem, and to an innumerable company of angels, to the general assembly and church of the firstborn (Hebrews 12:22-23).**

A Better Covenant with Better Promises

Hannah was under the Old Covenant, but we are under the New Covenant, which is a far better covenant. How much more should we be appropriating the promises of God that Jesus Himself purchased for us at the cross?

> **But now hath he [Jesus] obtained a more excellent ministry, by how much also he is the mediator of a better covenant, which was established upon better promises (Hebrews 8:6).**
>
> **Christ hath redeemed us from the curse of the law, being made a curse for us: for it is written, Cursed is every one that hangeth on a tree: that the blessing of Abraham might come**

on the Gentiles through Jesus Christ; that we might receive the promise of the Spirit through faith (Galatians 3:13-14).

And if ye be Christ's, then are ye Abraham's seed, and heirs according to the promise (Galatians 3:29).

We have been redeemed from the curse and released to the blessing. It's time for the people of God to rise up and, by faith, appropriate the blessings that Christ has purchased for us. Deuteronomy 28 tells us that we are to be the head and not the tail, above only and not beneath. Read the entire chapter of Deuteronomy 28 and make sure you are walking in all the blessings of the covenant. Also, make sure you are not allowing any of the curses of the Law mentioned in the last part of chapter 28 to operate in your life. God's people are to be the head and not the tail, above only and not beneath, a city set on a hill, the light of the world, triumphant, victorious, the redeemed of the Lord, etc.

A New Level of Grace

God's grace is about to take our prayer lives to the levels they were meant to be. This will facilitate the birthing of the *new thing* God promised to do in the earth. Let's take another look at the book of Ephesians, which confirms that there are many types of prayer.

Praying always with all prayer and supplication in the Spirit, and watching thereunto with all perseverance and supplication for all saints (Ephesians 6:18).

In the original Greek manuscript, this more accurately reads: "Praying with all manner or types of prayer being led by the Spirit."

Those who are truly close to God will feel His heartbeat and will be led by the Holy Spirit in their prayer lives. The Holy Spirit will lead and assist us in the many types of prayer including the prayer of faith and the prayer of intercession.

Going Higher

Many Christians today are trying to walk in the deep things of God without taking the necessary time and effort to build biblical,

A Strong Foundation

foundational truth in their lives. That would be like trying to build a skyscraper on a shallow foundation. The higher you want to build, the deeper and stronger your foundation must be. I see many today who want to walk in the high realms of God but have not taken the time to build a solid foundation of God's Word into their lives. For example, many today claim to be walking in the prophetic or even apostolic realms, but have bypassed or even look down upon the foundational teachings of faith. This is quite understandable, because many who currently claim to be leaders of *faith* or *word* movements have clearly gotten into extremism and error and have even confused *godliness* with *gain* (see 1 Timothy 6:5). But let's not throw out faith like throwing out the baby with the bathwater. Let's not get stuck in any movement, but let's not bypass essential doctrine either. According to Hebrews 6 "faith toward God" is a fundamental and absolutely essential foundation stone that we need before we are able to move into the deeper and meatier things of God.

Walking in holiness and purity is another foundational truth that many, who claim to be walking in the *deeper* things of God, tend to ignore or label as legalism. Like the faith or word movements, extremism and flat-out error have caused many to disregard the clear biblical mandate for holiness and purity. We can see from past moves of God that this foundational deficiency can allow ministries to become shipwrecked.

Full Speed Ahead

Like Hannah, we must be strong in faith and be able to pray by the leading and power of the Holy Spirit to allow something brand new and fresh to be birthed into the earth—something that will cause the upheaval and overturning of everything as we know it. If we are full of the Word of God, He can take the water of the Word that we have been diligent to feed on and turn it into wine, which speaks of life and power. Our prayer life will be weak, at best, if we are not taking the time to put the Word in us.

> **If ye abide in me, and my words abide in you, ye shall ask what ye will, and it shall be done unto you (John 15:7).**

HANNAH ROARS

Swift Advancement of God's Kingdom

As we fill up on God's Word and begin to pray and decree His Word, tremendous power will be released. This will result in tremendous advances of the will of God and the kingdom of God in our lives, in the church, and in the earth.

Hannah prophesied about the days we are now stepping into. After fervent prayer, she conceived and her baby eventually came forth. After the birth of Samuel, Hannah prayed again and prophesied about the days we now live in—a time when there would be a complete overturning of the kingdoms of this world. Hannah prophesied of a time when everything would be turned upside down and God's people would go from being the bottom to being the head and not the tail (see Deuteronomy 28).

Is This Your Vision for the Last Days?

We live in a day when Isaiah 2 and Micah 4 are beginning to be fulfilled, a day when the kingdom of God will be chief among all kingdoms. It's time for the cream to rise to the top. Everything is about to change. Are you ready? Let's get closer to God than ever before. It's time to draw near to God. It's time to seek His face. Look carefully at the following two Scriptures; remember, in the Scriptures, mountains often represent kingdoms.

> **And it shall come to pass in the last days, that the mountain of the Lord's house shall be established in the top of the mountains, and shall be exalted above the hills; and all nations shall flow unto it. And many people shall go and say, Come ye, and let us go up to the mountain of the Lord, to the house of the God of Jacob; and he will teach us of his ways, and we will walk in his paths: for out of Zion shall go forth the law, and the word of the Lord from Jerusalem (Isaiah 2:2-3).**

This is so important that the prophet Micah prophesies the exact same thing. The Bible declares that every important word is to be established by the mouth of two or three witnesses.

> **But in the last days it shall come to pass, that the mountain of the house of the Lord shall be established in the top of the**

A Strong Foundation

> mountains, and it shall be exalted above the hills; and people shall flow unto it. And many nations shall come, and say, Come, and let us go up to the mountain of the Lord, and to the house of the God of Jacob; and he will teach us of his ways, and we will walk in his paths: for the law shall go forth of Zion, and the word of the Lord from Jerusalem (Micah 4:1-2).

The above Scriptures declare that in the last days, the kingdom of God will rise to be chief above all the kingdoms of the earth—not the devil's kingdom, not the Antichrist's kingdom, but God's kingdom. Do you believe we are in the last days? Then perhaps we should quit preaching about the Antichrist and start preaching about Christ and His kingdom. The word *antichrist* is only used a few times in the books of first and second John. They proclaim antichrist as a spirit that was already at work during the times of the early church, not as a man who will rule the world in the last days. Again, the above Scriptures and many others are clear that in the last days the kingdom of God will be chief above all kingdoms and that nations will stream into it. This speaks of many people coming to know Christ, of a great harvest of souls coming into the kingdom. I know that in the last days there shall be great darkness and great distress. But the darkness and distress are just setting the stage for the people of God to arise and shine with the glory of God to make great advances for the kingdom of God.

> Arise, shine; for thy light is come, and the glory of the Lord is risen upon thee. For, behold, the darkness shall cover the earth, and gross darkness the people: but the Lord shall arise upon thee, and his glory shall be seen upon thee. And the Gentiles shall come to thy light, and kings to the brightness of thy rising (Isaiah 60:1–3).

The greatest days for God's people are upon us. It might look dark and hopeless. You may have suffered through great loss, trials, and apparent barrenness, but if you will cooperate with Him and learn to release His roar, God is about to arise within you and turn everything around. Hold on to His Word; it will hold you up. It will not fail you. There is much to learn to become like Christ and do His works. Grace and revelation are coming to equip and empower us to be the people of

God we are called to be. Through faith and endurance we will inherit the promises. Nowhere in the Scriptures are we told to be strong in our own strength. We are told in Ephesians 6:10 to be strong *"in the Lord"* and in the power of *"His might."*

> **That ye be not slothful, but followers of them who through faith and patience** [endurance] **inherit the promises (Hebrews 6:12).**

Chapter 3: The Story of Hannah

Chapter 3
The Story of Hannah

Darkness Abounds, but Can Not Prevail

Let's begin with 1 Samuel 1:1. Remember, these were the times of the judges; there were no kings. Eli was not only a priest but also a judge. The Bible says that Eli grew fat and his eyes grew dim and that his sons were corrupt. This is a type, or figure, of the fatness, excess, ease, blindness, and lack of vision we find today among many currently in leadership. It was not a good time. The Bible says there was very little *"Word of the Lord"* and *"no open vision"* (1 Samuel 3:1). It was a time when a child was named Ichabod, meaning *"the glory is departed"* (1 Samuel 4:21,22). His tangible presence had departed. The ark of the covenant had been stolen and the glory of God was gone.

This reminds me of the current state of the church. According to the New Testament, we are to walk in a glory that is greater than Moses walked in. The glory came down on the mountain where Moses met with God and the whole mountain shook and was burned. It was charred. Where is the glory in the midst of God's people today? Much is in disarray. Here we are in the 21st century and you can't even watch a news channel without being exposed to sin, defilement, and corruption. We need to have our remote controls in hand when we try to watch the news because some of the commercials are getting so gross and vile. Jesus said the church is to be the salt of the earth and light of the world. We are to have great influence in the earth—in politics, education, media, etc. The church of the Lord Jesus Christ has been in existence for nearly 2,000 years, and yet we still see wickedness and corruption abounding today, perhaps now more than ever.

HANNAH ROARS

Those in authority in America no longer show respect for the sanctity of life; our leaders are trying to turn our nation away from its foundation of being one nation under God. The Bible is clearly in disagreement with the present eclectic and compromised view that there are many roads that lead to God. We have heard a national leader say that we are no longer a Christian nation. This leader went on to say that we are now a nation of Hinduism, Islam, Judaism, and Christianity, but we're no longer just a narrow-minded Christian nation.

There had better be some Hannahs arising who are saying that there's something wrong. It's time for real change. We must recognize the need for a fresh move of God. We need a new breed of pure and godly leadership that will speak the uncompromised Word of God.

The Time Has Finally Come: Watchmen, Take Your Place!

"Now there was a certain man of Ramathaimzophim" (1 Samuel 1:1). *Ramathaimzophim*[3] means "double height of the watchers." I believe there is an alarm sounding for the watchmen, for intercessors, for those who watch and pray. There is a lot of talk about prophetic ministry today, but remember, true prophetic ministers are intercessors. The Bible says that true prophets will make intercession for the people and will speak in a way to turn people away from their iniquity (see Lamentations 2:14). The "double height" refers to the double portion, which is coming to those who have eyes to see and ears to hear. Continuing in verse 1: *"...of mount Ephraim"*; again, *Ephraim*[4] means "doubly fruitful, doubly blessed." This is interesting. Hannah is called to be doubly fruitful and yet has no fruit—no baby. This is so typical of God. In fact, this is a key to how He operates. This is a key to knowing His ways. We read in Romans 4:17 that God *"calleth those things which be not as though they were."*

The High Calling: The Birthing of the Man-child

Child of God, do you know that God has spoken fruitfulness over you? God has spoken success over you, God has spoken that you are

---

3. Strong, *Strong's Exhaustive Concordance*, H7436.
4. Ibid., H669.

The Story of Hannah

"the head and not the tail" by virtue of belonging to Christ and being Abraham's seed. *"And if ye be Christ's, then are ye Abraham's seed, and heirs according to the promise"* (Galatians 3:29). You are to be in places of authority and influence for the glory of God; you are to be ruling and reigning in life. But if you really look at the body of Christ, you've got to wonder where the fruit is.

Whether you are willing to admit it or not, every believer is walking in a state of barrenness to some degree. I know there are Christians, including many apostles and prophets out there, who think they have really arrived, but compared to the standard of the Scripture, and of Christ Himself, we must all humble ourselves and acknowledge the fact that we must come up higher. We have not yet attained to *"the high calling"* (Philippians 3:14), nor have we come to *"the measure of the stature of the fulness of Christ"* (Ephesians 4:13). I agree that there are many faithful, powerful, and anointed ministers and believers on the earth today, but I also know that no one has come to full maturity in Christ, nor has anyone yet been completely *"conformed to the image of his Son"* as referred to in Romans 8:29. But we will. That is our calling. All of Scripture will be fulfilled! Friends, no matter how long you have been saved or how anointed you are, there is more. Are you hungry for *all* that God has for you? Let's not be lukewarm or cavalier about our walk with the Lord, like the church of Laodicea in the book of Revelation. There are tremendous promises given to those who overcome lukewarmness and complacency.

> **So then because thou art lukewarm, and neither cold nor hot, I will spue thee out of my mouth. ...As many as I love, I rebuke and chasten: be zealous therefore, and repent. Behold, I stand at the door, and knock: if any man hear my voice, and open the door, I will come in to him, and will sup with him, and he with me. To him that overcometh will I grant to sit with me in my throne, even as I also overcame, and am set down with my Father in his throne (Revelation 3:16, 19–21).**

God has never condoned complacency in His people. He wants a people who are as passionate toward Him and His purposes as He is toward us.

HANNAH ROARS

Woe to them that are at ease in Zion (Amos 6:1).

Unprecedented Change Is Coming

We have not been walking in all the inheritance that Christ has provided for us. At times, it appears as if darkness has overtaken the light. But things are about to radically change. Isaiah 60:2 states, *"...darkness shall cover the earth, and gross darkness the people."* But now it's time for Hannah to give birth, and for the rest of Isaiah 60 to be fulfilled as His glory arises and is seen upon us. Isaiah 60:13 goes on to state, *"...and I will make the place of my feet glorious."* What is the place of His feet? Your feet are the part of your body that is in contact with the earth. The feet are the part of the body of Jesus that is still on the earth. If you're reading this, you are still on the earth, and you are not here by accident or by chance. You are a part of the *feet company* of God's people. God is going to make the place of His feet glorious. He's going to make you glorious. You might as well believe it. It's God's Word.

Hannah and Her Seed

Continuing on in 1 Samuel 1:1 *"...his* [Hannah's husband's] *name was Elkanah, the son of Jeroham the son of Elihu, the son of Tohu, the son of Zuph."* These names are all significant. *Elkanah* means "God has possessed or created."[5] This speaks of God's new creation—people who are completely in unity with Him. *Tohu* means "to be made lowly."[6] This speaks of humility. The amazing new thing that God is birthing will be birthed in and through a lowly, humble people—not from a prideful people who think they've got it all because they are rich, increased with goods, and need nothing. That's what the Laodicean church in Revelation 3 thought. In essence, the lukewarm church is saying, *I have shalom. I am complete. I have arrived.* They are crying "peace," which is the Hebrew word *shalom*. *Shalom* means wholeness, wellness, nothing missing, nothing lacking. But how whole is the church today? We need the glory of God back.

---

5. Strong, *Strong's Exhaustive Concordance*, H511.
6. Ibid., H8459.

The Story of Hannah

The name *Zuph*, in 1 Samuel 1:1, speaks of the honeycomb.[7] Remember when Jonathan ate the honey and *"his eyes were enlightened"* (1 Samuel 14:27)? In Ephesians 1:18, Paul prayed for the church, *"the eyes of your understanding being enlightened."* The church is about to receive fresh, clear vision. We are about to truly *"taste and see that the Lord is good!"* (See Psalm 34:8.)

Hannah Means "Grace"

First Samuel 1:2: *"And he had two wives; the name of the one was Hannah."* *Hannah* means "grace." Grace is about to birth something—not the works of the flesh, not talent, not connections, and not self-promotion. But make no mistake, grace is about to birth something that has never been seen before. Grace is God's undeserved, unmerited favor. Grace is God's empowerment and His ability working in us.

For it is God which worketh in you both to will and to do of his good pleasure (Philippians 2:13).

Right now, it may seem that Hannah (grace) has been somewhat unfruitful. But great change is coming. Look at the Old Testament men and women of God—they stopped the sun, parted the sea, slew giants, and walked in remarkable, manifest glory. Read about Joseph and the great wisdom he walked in. He was taken from the prison to the palace. He was placed in charge of all of Egypt (a type of the world). Get ready to walk clothed with the glory and the honor of God. Get ready to walk in a realm far beyond your abilities. Get ready to step out of yourself and into Him and His fullness.

Elkanah had two wives—Hannah and Peninnah. Peninnah had children, but Hannah had no children. Hannah was barren. Even though Hannah's name means grace, she was barren and fruitless. The name of Elkanah's other wife was Peninnah. *Peninnah* means "jewel." [8] Right now, it may appear that Peninnah is shining like a jewel, while Hannah appears to be unfruitful. But change is underway. Many of you may not appear to be shining right now; many of you, like Hannah, may appear to

---

7. Strong, *Strong's Exhaustive Concordance*, H6689.
8. Ibid, H6444.

be barren and fruitless. Perhaps you have experienced a failed business, a failed marriage, an unsuccessful ministry, unanswered prayers, etc. Don't give up! God is about to turn potential grace into operational grace. Hannah's turn is about to come.

Thou shalt arise, and have mercy upon Zion: for the time to favour her, yea, the set time, is come (Psalm 102:13).

God Meant It for Good

First Samuel 1:5 states that *"the Lord had shut up her* [Hannah's] *womb."* In his book, *Hints to Bible Interpretation,* Hebrew scholar Dr. Robert Young states that "the original Hebrew language did not have the necessary faculties by which to express the permissive tense of verbs, but only the causative tense of verbs." In other words, many verbs in the Old Testament that are translated into the English language in the causative tense should have actually been translated in the permissive tense. My point here is not to argue whether God had caused Hannah's womb to be shut, or simply permitted it to be shut. My point is this: whether the Lord caused it, or whether He allowed it, He was going to use it for good. He permitted it to bring something out of Hannah, to rouse and stir up something extraordinary in her. He was about to bring out the roar in her. Yes, indeed, He was about to roar through her. His purposes and desires were about to be birthed in the earth! Everything was about to change.

The Lord may have allowed your apparent failure or barrenness to make sure you would not settle for anything but God's best. It has been said by many that *good* is often the biggest enemy of *best*. I'm sure Peninnah's children were good. I'm sure the rest of the Israelite women were having—and raising—good children. But Israel needed something more than *good*. Israel needed transformation. It needed something extraordinary. It needed Hannah to birth a Samuel in the earth. It needed a Samuel who would deal with the corruption in the land and help usher in the Davidic kingdom, resulting in the silencing of all of Israel's enemies.

Maybe you've been allowed to fail or experience mediocrity and discontentment to stir up something in you that will no longer settle for

The Story of Hannah

mediocrity. The earth needs transformation. Romans 8 tells us that all of creation is groaning for the unveiling of the sons of God—for the birthing of a ministry that will drastically change the world as we know it and set creation free from the *"bondage of corruption"* (Romans 8:21).

The Game Changers Are Being Released

Jesus said in John 14:12: *"Verily, verily, I say unto you, He that believeth on me, the works that I do shall he do also; and greater works than these shall he do; because I go unto my Father."* According to Romans 8, there will be an unveiling of a company of people who will do more than heal the sick, raise the dead, and cast out demons. The greater works are about to be revealed. Jesus healed the sick and raised the dead, but they eventually died again.

One Day Is as a Thousand Years

And he said unto them, Go ye, and tell that fox, Behold, I cast out devils, and I do cures to day and to morrow, and the third day I shall be perfected (Luke 13:32).

Jesus cast out devils and healed people for more than two, literal, twenty-four-hour days. He was speaking of the 1,000-year days that the apostle Peter would later reveal:

But, beloved, be not ignorant of this one thing, that one day is with the Lord as a thousand years, and a thousand years as one day (2 Peter 3:8).

We are now entering into the third 1,000-year day of the church. Jesus said that on the third day He would be perfected. I know that Christ Jesus, the Head, is already perfect, but His church, which is called His body, is obviously not. The word *perfect* in Luke 13:32 comes from the Greek *teleioo*[9] which also means "finished, complete and fully mature." God is going to finish what He started in us! Aren't you glad?

---

9. W. E. Vine et al., *Vine's Complete Expository Dictionary of Old and New Testament Words* (Nashville, TN: Nelson, 1985).

HANNAH ROARS

Being confident of this very thing, that he which hath begun a good work in you will perform it until the day of Jesus Christ (Philippians 1:6).

The Bible delineates that there will be a people who do more than heal people and even more than raise the dead. There will be a people who come to full maturity and totally remove the curse! There will be a people who deliver creation from the bondage of corruption or decay. The second law of thermodynamics (which involves the universe and all that it contains being in a state of decay) will be reversed. All things will be restored back to God's original creation purpose.

For the earnest expectation of the creature [creation] **waiteth for the manifestation of the sons of God. ...Because the creature** [creation] **itself also shall be delivered from the bondage of corruption into the glorious liberty of the children of God (Romans 8:19, 21).**

The Temple Will Be Completed

What I am talking about may seem like an impossible, endless task, but the Word of God will be fulfilled. God's temple will be finished. Christ (the Head *and* His body) will come to complete maturity, fruition, and perfection. We can see this in type and shadow in Zechariah 4 concerning the rebuilding of the temple and all the difficulties and seemingly insurmountable obstacles that surrounded that task. Remember, you are the temple! Zechariah 4 is actually talking about the church, the true temple and dwelling place of God being finished (coming to full maturity).

Then he answered and spake unto me, saying, This is the word of the Lord unto Zerubbabel, saying, Not by might, nor by power, but by my spirit, saith the Lord of hosts. Who art thou, O great mountain [obstacle]**? before Zerubbabel thou shalt become a plain: and he shall bring forth the headstone** [the headstone was the finishing piece] **thereof with shoutings, crying, Grace, grace unto it (Zechariah 4:6-7).**

The Story of Hannah

Did you get that? God is going to finish the work in His body, His true dwelling place. And how is He going to do it? By His Spirit with shouts of "Grace, Grace!" What does this have to do with Hannah? Hannah, in Hebrew, means "grace"! His body, which is His church, will come to maturity by an unprecedented release of His grace.

It's Time to Pray for Rain

Ask ye of the Lord rain in the time of the latter rain; so the Lord shall make bright clouds, and give them showers of rain, to every one grass in the field (Zechariah 10:1).

Any farmer knows that nothing can turn around a struggling crop and help it grow and come to full maturity better and faster than the abundance of rain. And that's exactly what God has in store for you and me. God is going to pour His Spirit out upon His people in an unprecedented way.

Be glad then, ye children of Zion, and rejoice in the Lord your God: for he hath given you the former rain moderately, and he will cause to come down for you the rain, the former rain, and the latter rain in the first month (Joel 2:23).

Chapter 4: The Feast of Tabernacles

Chapter 4
The Feast of Tabernacles

Beyond First Fruits

He will cause to come down for you the rain, the former rain, and the latter rain in the first month (Joel 2:23).

The first month, as mentioned in the above verse, refers to the time of the Feast of Tabernacles. The Feast of Tabernacles, or Booths, was the third and final major feast of the year in Israel. The Feast of Tabernacles was the feast of the full and final harvest of the year. The first two major feasts, Passover and Pentecost, were both partial (first fruits) harvests. The Feast of Passover was the first fruits of the barley harvest and the Feast of Pentecost was the first fruits of the wheat harvest. All of this has significant meaning for us today.

The Feast of Tabernacles was not a partial (first fruits) harvest. The Feast of Tabernacles was the complete harvest of the agricultural year. At the time of Tabernacles, all the wheat was mature and ready for harvesting, not just the first fruits, as at Pentecost. The time of the Feast of Tabernacles was also the time of the complete fruit harvest coming to maturity. Aren't you glad that the fruit of the Spirit will come to maturity in Christ's body at this time, the time of harvest? Don't be discouraged at the chastening and pruning of the Lord. He has a harvest of good fruit in mind.

The Corn, the Wine, and the Oil

The Feast of Tabernacles was also the time of the full wheat harvest, the olive harvest, and the fruit harvest (which included the grapes). Keep in mind that the olives were used to make oil and the grapes were used to make wine. The words *corn* (which refers to any grain, including wheat), *wine*, and *oil* are used together around eighteen times in the Bible. When these words are used together they signify and indicate the time of the Feast of Tabernacles. The Feast of Tabernacles occurred at the time of the harvest, or as Jesus called it, the end of the age—a time when everything comes to maturity.

From Pentecost to Tabernacles

We have experienced a wonderful harvest of Pentecostal blessings during the church age, but Pentecost is not Tabernacles. According to Leviticus 23:16-17, Pentecost, in type and shadow, involved a celebration which included the use of two loaves of bread with leaven (yeast). Yeast (leaven) in the Bible is often a type or shadow of sin. As wonderful as the last 2,000 years of the Pentecostal church age has been, it has been laden with sin, imperfection, and immaturity. Even the most glorious revivals and awakenings in church history have been tainted with leaven. The fruit of the Spirit has not come to full maturity in Christ's body because we have not yet experienced the former and latter rains that are now at the door.

> **That I will give you the rain of your land in his due season, the first rain and the latter rain, that thou mayest gather in thy corn, and thy wine, and thine oil (Deuteronomy 11:14).**

Whether you can admit it or not, compared to what's coming, we have all been in somewhat of a drought.

> **And I called for a drought upon the land, and upon the mountains, and upon the corn, and upon the new wine, and upon the oil, and upon that which the ground bringeth forth, and upon men, and upon cattle, and upon all the labour of the hands (Haggai 1:11).**

The Feast of Tabernacles has indeed eluded us. The spiritual fulfillment of the Feast of Tabernacles has yet to be completely fulfilled. But the turnaround is here. It's a new day. It's a new season. Joel saw and prophesied the turnaround for God's people.

The Feast of Tabernacles

The field is wasted, the land mourneth; for the corn is wasted: the new wine is dried up, the oil languisheth (Joel 1:10).

Joel saw the lack. But he also saw and prophesied the turnaround.

Yea, the Lord will answer and say unto his people, Behold, I will send you corn, and wine, and oil, and ye shall be satisfied therewith: and I will no more make you a reproach among the heathen (Joel 2:19).

As we will see, Hannah also prophesied of this ultimate turnaround and overturn in history. Remember, history is *His story*. And His story is not finished yet. The climax of the history of the ages is now upon us.

Up until now, the "high calling" previously mentioned has escaped our grasp. But remember, Pentecost was never meant to be the complete harvest. The Feast of Tabernacles is the feast of the full harvest, which includes the fruit harvest. God is a God of times and seasons. And the time for the full maturity of the harvest is finally at hand.

Again, the Feast of Tabernacles was celebrated in the fall, at the time of the full harvest, which occurred at the end of one year and the beginning of a new year. (Israel actually had two New Years—a religious New Year, which began in the spring, and a civil/agricultural New Year, which began in the fall. For the purpose of this study, we are talking about the civil/agricultural New Year which began in the fall, during the Feast of Tabernacles.) Jesus said that the harvest was at the end of the age. And because, as many believe, we are in the time of the harvest (the end of the church age), we can surely expect Joel 2:23 to be fulfilled with an unprecedented outpouring of the Holy Spirit many times greater than even the early church experienced.

In Palestine, the former (or early) rains came in the fall to prepare the soil for planting and the seeds for germination and initial growth. The latter rains came later in the season during the springtime. The purpose of the latter rains was to bring the crop to full maturity (remember, you're the crop).

HANNAH ROARS

Did Joel Flunk Meteorology Class?

Because Joel had spent his life in Palestine, I'm sure he was not ignorant of the rain patterns of the region. He knew that the heavier latter rains did not come in the fall, at the time of the Feast of Tabernacles. But that's exactly what he said would occur. Look back to that verse.

Joel was stating that in the first month, the season of Tabernacles, the time of the harvest (the end of the age), we will experience the greatest outpouring of the Spirit of God that the world has ever seen! The latter rain is actually God Himself in our midst in His fullness. Here's another third-day prophecy:

> **Come, and let us return unto the Lord: for he hath torn, and he will heal us; he hath smitten, and he will bind us up. After two days will he revive us: in the third day he will raise us up, and we shall live in his sight. Then shall we know, if we follow on to know the Lord: his going forth is prepared as the morning; and he shall come unto us as the rain, as the latter and former rain unto the earth (Hosea 6:1–3).**

Did you catch that? The Lord is coming to us as the former and latter rain. It's all about Him. I love signs, wonders, and miracles, but the essence of the latter rain is the Lord Himself, not just spiritual phenomena. We're about to get excited about the Lord as never before. We're about to return to our first love. And all ministry and expansion of the kingdom will flow from knowing and loving Him.

If...

Did you notice the conditional word *if* in the above Scripture? Hosea 6 says *"if we return"* and *"follow on to know the Lord"* then He will come to us as the rain. We, like Hannah, have a part to play in receiving what the Lord desires for us. If Hannah hadn't been proactive but had remained complacent, she would have remained barren. It's time to seek the Lord. Like Hannah, it's time to release the *roar* so that the Lord's highest purposes for us can be fulfilled.

I wonder how many Christians are in jobs they were never called to do, cities they were never sent to, and churches that don't even

The Feast of Tabernacles

slightly resemble the New Testament churches in the book of Acts. Are you satisfied with the level of the anointing you are walking in? Are you satisfied with your level of intimacy with the Lord? If not, then don't give up. Pray! Seek God! Draw near to Him and He will draw near to you (see James 4:8). Hannah never gave up. Will you? God will answer. It may seem like it's a long time coming, but when the answer comes, it will come swiftly and suddenly and will be above all that you could ask or think.

> **And he spake a parable unto them to this end, that men ought always to pray, and not to faint…And shall not God avenge his own elect, which cry day and night unto him, though he bear long with them? I tell you that he will avenge them speedily. Nevertheless when the Son of man cometh, shall he find faith on the earth? (Luke 18:1, 7-8)**

> **Sow to yourselves in righteousness, reap in mercy; break up your fallow ground: for it is time to seek the Lord, till he come and rain righteousness upon you (Hosea 10:12).**

The Lord's Prayer: More Than a Religious Exercise

> **After this manner therefore pray ye: Our Father which art in heaven, Hallowed be thy name. Thy kingdom come, Thy will be done in earth, as it is in heaven (Matthew 6:9-10).**

Jesus' prayer will actually be answered. God's kingdom will come in its fullness and in all of its glory. His will is going to be done on earth as it is in heaven. And His church has a great part to play in this. Look at what Jesus said about His church, His body.

> **And upon this rock I will build my church; and the gates of hell shall not prevail against it. And I will give unto thee the keys of the kingdom of heaven: and whatsoever thou shalt bind** [forbid] **on earth shall be bound in heaven: and whatsoever thou shalt loose** [allow] **on earth shall be loosed in heaven (Matthew 16:18-19).**

HANNAH ROARS

What tremendous authority the church has been given. And we are about to awaken to that reality like never before. The kingdom of God is at hand.

Ready or Not, Here I Come!

The Lord is coming just as He said and so is the fullness of His kingdom on earth. Unbelievers, and even many who claim to be Christians, seem unaware of the great change that is upon us.

Knowing this first, that there shall come in the last days scoffers, walking after their own lusts, and saying, Where is the promise of his coming? for since the fathers fell asleep, all things continue as they were from the beginning of the creation (2 Peter 3:3-4).

It's time to prepare the way of the Lord. It is God's desire for His church, like Hannah and her son, Samuel, to be used to prepare the way for and even help usher in the kingdom. Now is the time to boldly proclaim and demonstrate the gospel of the kingdom. Jesus said to occupy until He comes (see Luke 19:13). The word translated *occupy* means to "do business."[10] We are to be about our Father's business. Get ready to get off the sidelines and into the game. We, like Hannah, are going to learn how to change our circumstances and, in turn, bring great change to the earth. If we follow the lessons of Hannah, we can go from being *under the circumstances* to changing and dominating the circumstances, not only in our own lives, but in the earth as well. Remember, Jesus said He would give His church the keys of the kingdom to bind and loose on earth. God is quite capable of ushering in His kingdom on the earth by Himself, but He won't do it without His church, His body. Every good father enjoys seeing his children develop. And our heavenly Father delights in seeing us grow in ability, character, power, and authority. It actually brings Him much pleasure.

Fear not, little flock; for it is your Father's good pleasure to give you the kingdom (Luke 12:32).

---

10. Strong, *Strong's Exhaustive Concordance*, G4231.

The Feast of Tabernacles

Original Intent

Let's take a look at the idea of *original intent*. According to the book of origins, that is, the book of Genesis, man was created in the image and likeness of God. Man was created to fill the earth, rule the earth, and subdue the earth. Man was not originally created to be subdued or be dominated by circumstances or failure. Jesus is called the last Adam, and He came to restore all that the first Adam lost in the fall and beyond. Hannah learned how to turn failure and barrenness into victory and triumph. We are told that through Christ we too can rule and reign in life. We too are called to turn adversity into triumph. Look at this verse closely; this is God's Word and His will for you.

> **For if by one man's offence** [Adam's sin] **death reigned by one; much more they which receive abundance of grace and of the gift of righteousness shall reign in life by one, Jesus Christ (Romans 5:17).**

It's time to reign in life! That's now! The Amplified Bible says *"reign as kings in life."*

> **And hast made us unto our God kings and priests: and we shall reign on the earth (Revelation 5:10).**

God has made you a king. Take your place. Jesus is King of kings and Lord of lords. You are a king and He is King over you. Don't let the enemy or circumstances dominate you. You were not created in His image for failure or defeat. Rise up and take the name of Jesus and the authority He has given you and put the enemy on the run.

> **Submit yourselves therefore to God. Resist the devil, and he will flee from you (James 4:7).**

Hannah didn't settle for defeat, shame, and barrenness, and neither should you.

The God of Armies

Let's get back to Hannah's story. Hannah's husband, Elkanah, was a godly man. His name, *Elkanah*, means God's possession and God's creation. This speaks of God's new creation in the earth. *"And this man went up out of his city yearly to worship and to sacrifice unto the Lord of hosts in Shiloh"* (1 Samuel 1:3). This phrase, *Lord of Hosts*, is one of many names used for God in the Bible. It means "God of Armies." It is significant that 1 Samuel is the first place in the Scripture that this name is used. God is about to, once again, reveal Himself as the God of Armies in the bringing forth of his people out of captivity and barrenness. It will not be business as usual. We are about to see divine, heavenly intervention in the earth on an unprecedented scale.

It's time to get a bigger view of God. Our God reigns. It's time to magnify the Lord and what He is doing in the earth, not the enemy and his futile plans. Jesus is the Head of all principalities and powers, and the earth belongs to Him.

For in Him [Christ] **dwelleth all the fulness of the Godhead bodily. And ye are complete in Him, which is the head of all principality and power (Colossians 2:9-10).**

The earth is the Lord's, and the fulness thereof; the world, and they that dwell therein (Psalm 24:1).

Let's never forget who's ultimately in charge—Jesus Christ, the Head—and His body will have the last word. I would encourage you to read all of Psalm 2. It speaks of the complete overturning of all things as we know them. As we will see later on, Hannah also prophesied of this upheaval in amazing detail.

Why do the heathen rage, and the people imagine a vain thing? The kings of the earth set themselves, and the rulers take counsel together, against the Lord, and against his anointed, saying, Let us break their bands asunder, and cast away their cords from us. He that sitteth in the heavens shall laugh: the Lord shall have them in derision. Then shall he speak unto them in his wrath, and vex them in his sore displeasure. ...Ask of me, and I shall give thee the heathen for thine inheritance, and the uttermost parts of the earth for thy possession. Thou shalt break them with

The Feast of Tabernacles

a rod of iron; thou shalt dash them in pieces like a potter's vessel (Psalm 2:1–5, 8-9).

Later we will discuss in detail how our prayers have a tremendous part to play in the release of God's dominion.

Shiloh: The Place of Rest

And this man [Hannah's husband] **went up out of his city yearly to worship and to sacrifice unto the Lord of hosts in Shiloh (1 Samuel 1:3).**

Hannah and her husband went to Shiloh. *Shiloh* means "the place of rest." Are you ready to enter into God's rest? A place where you are no longer struggling, no longer striving. There is a striving in the spirit that is biblical, but I am speaking of entering into that finished work of Jesus, where it's no longer you working but Him working in you. We need to be careful that we are not mistaking spiritual laziness and apathy with the true rest of God. To enter into the genuine rest of God, you must labor. I'm not talking about laboring or striving in the flesh, but laboring in the Spirit.

Let us labour therefore to enter into that rest, lest any man fall after the same example of unbelief (Hebrews 4:11).

Hannah is a good example of a person who wasn't spiritually lazy or complacent. People around her, including her husband and Eli the priest, did not understand her spiritual fervor. But she would not settle for unfruitfulness. She had a good life in many ways. Her husband greatly loved her and she was well provided for. But something deep within her would not let her be satisfied with just having a good life. In fact, having a good life can sometimes be the worst enemy of entering into God's perfect will. But Hannah knew there was a higher call for her life than just being blessed. So she pressed in for God's best. Without her spiritual zeal and pursuit of God, Hannah would have never been used of Him to birth the *new thing* into the earth that God so desired.

HANNAH ROARS

Aggressive Prayer

> **Confess your faults one to another, and pray one for another, that ye may be healed. The effectual fervent prayer of a righteous man availeth much (James 5:16).**

There is a labor in the Spirit that we must enter into. It involves a passion for God's Word and fervent prayer. It involves a zeal to do His perfect will in our lives.

> **Now I beseech you, brethren, for the Lord Jesus Christ's sake, and for the love of the Spirit, that ye strive together with me in your prayers to God for me (Romans 15:30).**

> **Not as though I had already attained, either were already perfect: but I follow after, if that I may apprehend that for which also I am apprehended of Christ Jesus. Brethren, I count not myself to have apprehended: but this one thing I do, forgetting those things which are behind, and reaching forth unto those things which are before, I press toward the mark for the prize of the high calling of God in Christ Jesus (Philippians 3:12–14).**

The Zeal of the Lord

If you are going to be zealous about fulfilling the high call of God for your life, you had better prepare for misunderstanding, even mockery. But regardless of the opposition, it is time to be more like God, and God is full of zeal! Let's come up to His level and not try to bring Him down to ours.

> **For the zeal of thine house hath eaten me up; and the reproaches of them that reproached thee are fallen upon me (Psalm 69:9).**

> **And his disciples remembered that it was written, The zeal of thine house hath eaten me up (John 2:17).**

> **My zeal hath consumed me, because mine enemies have forgotten thy words (Psalm 119:139).**

The Feast of Tabernacles

Of the increase of his government and peace there shall be no end, upon the throne of David, and upon his kingdom, to order it, and to establish it with judgment and with justice from henceforth even for ever. The zeal of the Lord of hosts will perform this (Isaiah 9:7).

We are about to see the zeal of the Lord like never before. He is going to come through for us in a big way. Let's prepare for these changes!

The Lord shall go forth as a mighty man, he shall stir up jealousy like a man of war: he shall cry, yea, roar; he shall prevail against his enemies. I have long time holden my peace; I have been still, and refrained myself: now will I cry like a travailing woman; I will destroy and devour at once. I will make waste mountains and hills, and dry up all their herbs; and I will make the rivers islands, and I will dry up the pools (Isaiah 42:13–15).

A Changing of the Guard

Eli was Israel's priest and judge. His name means "ascension"—he was called of God, but fell into apathy. With the exception of his unwillingness to discipline his sons, you can't see much wrong with Eli. But it's not always the big sins that take God's people down. King Solomon said it is the little foxes that spoil the vines (see Song of Solomon 2:15). And the so-called little sins in our lives can spoil the harvest that God desires for us. Eli's sons, however, were overtly corrupt to the core. Eli found out that his sons were committing fornication on temple grounds, taking bribes, taking the offerings by force, and using for themselves even that which was to be dedicated to the Lord. Eli knew about these egregious sins, but just slapped his sons on the wrist instead of really putting his foot down and removing them from their place of influence. The Bible says that because he esteemed his sons more than the Lord, God would cut off Eli and his sons from the priesthood forever and that their sins would not be atoned for forever. Wow!

Let's learn from this. When we see unrepentant sin and corruption, we had better confront it. Because Eli esteemed his sons more than the Lord, the judgment of God would be upon his house. We must make certain that we are not putting anything, including loved ones, above the Lord and His will for our lives. I have observed many people today who won't go after the will of God for their lives for fear of stirring up misunderstanding or opposition from their spouse or loved ones. People will not always understand the plan and call of God for our lives, but we had better not let that get in the way of obeying Him. Doing so could disqualify us from truly following the Lord.

Do I seek to please men? for if I yet pleased men, I should not be the servant of Christ (Galatians 1:10).

This Scripture is pretty clear. We cannot serve God if we are seeking the approval of men. We had better be the man or woman of God we are called to be and not esteem the love, approval, and acceptance of others more than we esteem the Lord. Oftentimes when we attempt to obey the leading of the Lord for our lives, opposition will arise on several fronts. Jesus Himself promised us this.

Approved Building Materials

Wise governments require that building materials be tested and approved before they can be used in dwellings. The Bible says that we are living stones being used in the building of God's house. And you can be sure that God is a wise master builder who tests His building materials. The book of Revelation tells us that those who overcome can be made to be pillars in His house. He is looking for followers who can hold up under the weight and pressure that inevitably comes with the expansion of His kingdom, not those who will be swayed by circumstances and by the pressure of the people like King Saul was. It seems that some of the hardest tests for some to pass are the money tests and the family tests.

If any man come to me, and hate [love less] **not his father, and mother, and wife, and children, and brethren, and sisters, yea, and his own life also, he cannot be my disciple.** *And whosoever doth not bear his cross, and come after me, cannot be my disciple.* **...So likewise, whosoever he be of you that forsaketh not all that he hath, he cannot be my disciple (Luke 14:26-27, 33,** emphasis mine**).**

The Feast of Tabernacles

Jesus said that we can expect opposition, even from loved ones.

Think not that I am come to send peace on earth: I came not to send peace, but a sword. For I am come to set a man at variance against his father, and the daughter against her mother, and the daughter in law against her mother in law. And a man's foes shall be they of his own household. He that loveth father or mother more than me is not worthy of me: and he that loveth son or daughter more than me is not worthy of me (Matthew 10:34–37).

The Scriptures instruct us to put the Lord so exceedingly first that our love for anything else seems like hatred. When we love the Lord above our family, we will be able to love our family more than we ever could have on our own. Some of you may be going through maltreatment for attempting to serve the Lord. You may be wondering what's wrong with you. Instead you must realize that persecutions and hardships are promised to every true believer. That's the way you enter into the kingdom—through much tribulation.

Confirming the souls of the disciples, and exhorting them to continue in the faith, and that we must through much tribulation enter into the kingdom of God (Acts 14:22).

Blessed are they which are persecuted for righteousness' sake: for theirs is the kingdom of heaven (Matthew 5:10).

Just be sure you are suffering for righteousness' *sake* and not for your own stubbornness or for unbecoming or bad behavior or even so-called religious behavior. The religious leaders mentioned in Matthew 23 provide us with an example of unprofitable "religious" behavior. They had an outward appearance of righteousness but were full of hatred, bitterness, spiritual pride, hypocrisy, self-righteousness, and false judgment.

Let's not make Eli's mistake by putting anything or any person above God. Eli should have said to his sons, *I'm the judge here and I have the authority to throw you in prison. Regardless of whether you are family or not, I cannot allow you to bring corruption to this nation.*

HANNAH ROARS

But because Eli did not put his foot down and allowed corruption and worldliness in God's house, God judged him.

No More Canaanites in God's House

Eli's two sons were Hophni and Phinehas. The meanings of their names are rather interesting. *Hophni* means "pugilist, fighter" and *Phinehas* means "mouth of brass" or "serpent's mouth." We have far too many fighters and judgmental mouths in the church, but this will soon be dealt with. God is cleansing His temple once again. True holiness is about to make a comeback.

> **In that day shall there be upon the bells of the horses, holiness unto the Lord; and the pots in the Lord's house shall be like the bowls before the altar. Yea, every pot in Jerusalem and in Judah shall be holiness unto the Lord of hosts: and all they that sacrifice shall come and take of them, and seethe therein: and in that day there shall be no more the Canaanite in the house of the Lord of hosts (Zechariah 14:20-21).**

Double for Your Trouble

> **And when the time was that Elkanah offered, he gave to Peninnah his wife, and to all her sons and her daughters, portions: but unto Hannah he gave a worthy portion; for he loved Hannah: but the Lord had shut up her womb (1 Samuel 1:4-5).**

Some translations say that Elkanah gave Hannah a double portion, but the word translated "worthy" portion in Hebrew also means "passionate" portion. God wants passionate lovers. He doesn't want His people to be laid back, lukewarm, and lackadaisical. Elkanah gave a double portion to Hannah because he loved her; but verse 5 goes on to state, *"but the Lord had shut up her womb."* As we will see, the Lord did not intend barrenness to be her ultimate destiny.

Come Up Higher

If we are honest, we will admit that the Lord's people are experiencing some degree of barrenness today. God's plan, vision, and passion for us

The Feast of Tabernacles

have not yet been completely fulfilled in our lives. Many are humbly acknowledging that our families, businesses, ministries, and indeed our walk with the Lord are not at the level where they should be. God's calling for His church, His bride, is a high calling. Up until now, that high calling has eluded us. Even the most powerful and anointed ministers today have not successfully revived the church and awakened the nations. Even the revivals and great awakenings of the past, as powerful as they were, have been limited and temporary. What is about to be birthed will change all of that.

Rousing the Roar

The Lord may have caused that sense of dissatisfaction in you to arouse something extraordinary out of you. God often leads His people to a wilderness or Red Sea, but not for the purpose of remaining there. God may have allowed you to come to a place of barrenness and adversity to bring the lion's roar out of you as He did with Hannah, so you too can birth something truly extraordinary in the earth.

Some things can only come through adversity. The Bible says we enter into the kingdom through much tribulation. It seems that God's people have been going through trials, tests, and adversities on a grand scale. I believe God is allowing these adversities for a higher purpose. The enemy would hope that these wilderness and Red Sea experiences would destroy you, but God is allowing adversity for the purpose of birthing something new in you and through you—something that has never been seen before in the earth. This is not false hope or sensationalism. I believe we are not even capable of exaggerating the coming move of God.

You do not have to stay in that place of adversity or barrenness forever. You are destined to overcome. Like an eagle, you can learn how to stretch out those wings and use the winds of the storm that is buffeting you to rise higher than you have ever been before. Many have been told in this hour that the *perfect storm* is coming. This storm will indeed bring destruction to many; the Word of God is clear on that. The storm is not going to take God's covenant children down though. If you learn how to release the roar, as Hannah did, the winds of adversity and hardship are actually going to lift you up and cause you to learn how to overcome and soar.

Take Your Rightful Place

The Scriptures declare that you have been given great authority and are called to reign and rule over the enemy and his lying, adverse circumstances. So take your place in the heavenlies at the right hand of God. Because you have been raised with Christ far above all the power of the enemy, you can look down at the enemy and laugh and declare, *you are under my feet.*

And hath [past tense] **raised us up together, and made us sit together in heavenly places in Christ Jesus (Ephesians 2:6).**

Make sure you are walking by faith and not by sight. Don't base your faith on past or current experiences alone. I know that there are times or seasons when circumstances make it appear that the Word of God isn't true. But Satan is a liar. Get your eyes off the circumstances and onto God's Word.

They that observe lying vanities forsake their own mercy (Jonah 2:8).

Base your beliefs on God's Word, not on your circumstances or experiences. Let's not lower God's Word down to our experience. Let's learn the keys that will bring our experiences and circumstances up to the level of God's Word. Many Christians today are basing their beliefs on their experiences rather than God's Word. Our belief systems and doctrines must come from the Word of God. Scripture (not experience) has been given to us for doctrine.

All scripture is given by inspiration of God, and is profitable for doctrine, for reproof, for correction, for instruction in righteousness: that the man of God may be perfect, thoroughly furnished unto all good works (2 Timothy 3:16-17).

Base your faith on the Word of God and hold out for His covenant promises as Hannah did, even in the midst of contrary circumstances. Make sure you are doing your part of the covenant by giving the Lord your all

The Feast of Tabernacles

and by seeking to follow His perfect will for your life. Don't give up. Don't throw in the towel because of adversity. God has allowed it to be there to help lift you to a whole new level. When you walk by faith, people might think you are a bit crazy. Like Hannah, your mourning will be turned to gladness. You are about to come out of the wilderness with shouts of joy. Even the Lord implied in one of His parables that true faith would be rare when He returns.

> **And he spake a parable unto them to this end, that men ought always to pray, and not to faint. …Nevertheless when the Son of man cometh, shall he find faith on the earth? (Luke 18:1, 8)**

True faith may be rare at the end of the age, but let's determine that He will find it in us. The Lord can save by many or by few (see 1 Samuel 14:6). Scripture usually indicates that the Lord enjoys saving by few; look at the story of Gideon. He reduced Gideon's army to only 300 warriors. History has shown, and the Bible declares, that a relatively small number with a powerful anointing can bring great deliverance. Ultimately, all of creation has been waiting for this, and this ultimate deliverance will come from God's children.

> **Because the creature** [creation] **itself also shall be delivered from the bondage of corruption into the glorious liberty of the children of God (Romans 8:21).**

It's time for deliverers to ascend the mountain. It's time to come up higher.

> **And saviours** [other translations say "deliverers"] **shall come up on mount Zion to judge the mount of Esau; and the kingdom shall be the Lord's (Obadiah 21).**

God often brings us to a place of total dependency on Him, a place where we must seek Him and learn to press and push to bring forth His desired plans. He wants us to learn how to take the kingdom by force and press into realms that we never knew existed. He is bringing His people to a place where we cannot rely on our own abilities, talents, or

HANNAH ROARS

resources. He is bringing us to another Red Sea: a place where we will learn to walk in the power of His might and strength.

Now the just shall live by faith: but if any man draw back, my soul shall have no pleasure in him (Hebrews 10:38).

Chapter 5: Hannah Roars

Chapter 5
Hannah Roars

Time to Roar

Now let's get to the part of Hannah's story found in 1 Samuel 1:6 that explains what I mean by *Hannah roars*. As I explained in the introduction, Hannah's response to her situation led her into an aggressive stance in prayer—one in which she stood strong on the covenantal promises of her Lord. She actually roared in prayer—pouring herself out before God, knowing He would hear her and answer. Her adversity had pushed her into this place where she stood firm and roared! Her prayer brought forth great change that would affect the nation of Israel for all time. Hannah is a model for us of what to do in our day to bring forth God's will again in the face of our own adversity and apparent lack of fruit.

At times, I have been tempted to look in the natural as I look at God's people, including myself, and wonder: *God, what are You doing? How long are You going to allow Your people to be reproached?*

> **Let the priests, the ministers of the Lord, weep between the porch and the altar, and let them say, Spare thy people, O Lord, and give not thine heritage to reproach, that the heathen should rule over them: wherefore should they say among the people, Where is their God? (Joel 2:17).**

It's time to get serious with God. It's time to seek Him with new vigor. Let's realize that He has given us great influence with Him. He has made us to be kings and priests.

HANNAH ROARS

And hast made us unto our God kings and priests: and we shall reign on the earth (Revelation 5:10).

Priests can intercede on behalf of the people to bring God's intervention, and kings have the authority to bring great change in earthly realms. Start praying as never before. Start decreeing as never before. Use the keys of the kingdom that have been given to you (Matthew 16).

Where the word of a king [that's you] **is, there is power: and who may say unto him, What doest thou? (Ecclesiastes 8:4).**

Take your place as kings and priests. Release the anointed spoken word.

Thou shalt also decree a thing, and it shall be established unto thee: and the light shall shine upon thy ways (Job 22:28).

Adversity has been put in our paths to make us thunder, to make us roar, to let the lion of the tribe of Judah come up out of us, be provoked out of us, be stirred out of us, so that He comes forth and we learn to rule and reign with Him.

Are you in adversity, trials, or tests? Going from adversity to triumph, from barrenness to fruitfulness, will not happen automatically. It's important that you respond properly to adversity. Many respond improperly and go into a shell; they become black holes, they become self-centered and self-absorbed. Resist self-pity and depression. If we truly believe the Scriptures and what they declare about our glorious inheritance in Christ and the victory that He has purchased for us, then we must admit that we have relatively little to be depressed about. Few have gone through the hardships and persecutions of the apostle Paul. He called stonings, beatings, imprisonments, and shipwrecks "light afflictions." Paul walked by faith and not by sight. He focused on the glory, not the grief. What are you looking at?

For I reckon that the sufferings of this present time are not worthy to be compared with the glory which shall be revealed in us (Romans 8:18).

Hannah Roars

All of us have been tempted with self-pity and depression to some degree. Depression can be one of the highest forms of selfishness and self-centeredness. It can even open a door for sickness and disease to come into your body. One way out of self-pity and depression is to put your focus outward. Focus on how you can help others, forget about yourself, and do the ministry of Jesus by doing good and helping others. Be careful that adversity doesn't put you in a black hole and cause you to be self-centered. Don't get into the "woe is me" syndrome and send out subtle invitations for others to join your pity party. Instead, rise up and keep company with people who will not pity you but will help bring the Lion of the Lord out of you. Let adversity bring the roar out of you. I agree there have been some hard times in the body of Christ, but God wants to release His Lion in you. Do not succumb to the enemy. Make a decision not to get offended, not to get bitter; but to respond properly and to get better. Many people in adversity start to complain and grumble; be careful, because that behavior can lead to your defeat. You may lose your reward and have to start all over again. I don't know about you, but I am tired of going through the same tests over and over again. Let's pass the tests by being doers of the Word, so that we can move into the fruitful life God has for us.

Behold, I come quickly: hold that fast which thou hast, that no man take thy crown (Revelation 3:11).

I don't want to start over again. I've had to do that too many times. Instead of grumbling and complaining, I'm going to start thanking God and praising Him. That's what the Bible instructs us to do. That's being a doer of the Word and not just a hearer. By the way, when does the breakthrough usually come? Usually, when the attack of discouragement is the strongest. Let's walk by faith in God's Word. We must learn to get out of the flesh and quit walking by sight; the enemy is allowed to eat *dust*, which is a type of the flesh. Rise to the surface and say, *Enough of this pity! I believe God. If God's Word is true, which it is, then I have nothing to be discouraged about.*

I want to do what David did at Ziklag when all seemed lost. In reality he was just moments away from his enemy, Saul, being destroyed. David was moments away from the kingdom, but he had just lost everything—

HANNAH ROARS

including his wives and children and the wives and children of all the men who were following him. Instead of being discouraged, the Bible says that David encouraged himself in the Lord. Perhaps that's when he wrote Psalm 103. In this psalm, David is actually addressing his own soul—his own mind, will, and emotions. He is saying: *Hey, soul, don't be depressed! Praise the Lord! Remember **all** of His covenant blessings and benefits!* We will have to be like David and take hold of our thoughts and remind ourselves of God's covenant blessings. This is being a doer of the Word.

> **Bless the Lord, O my soul: and all that is within me, bless his holy name. Bless the Lord, O my soul, and forget not all his benefits: who forgiveth all thine iniquities; who healeth all thy diseases; who redeemeth thy life from destruction; who crowneth thee with lovingkindness and tender mercies; who satisfieth thy mouth with good things; so that thy youth is renewed like the eagle's. The Lord executeth righteousness and judgment for all that are oppressed (Psalm 103:1–6).**

There is a miracle in your mouth. Fill your mouth with God's Word and with praise. This combination of speaking God's Word and releasing praise unto Him is a key that will bring defeat to the adversary every time. The following verses highlight the power of combining God's Word with praise.

> **Let the high praises of God be in their mouth, and a two-edged sword in their hand; to execute vengeance upon the heathen, and punishments upon the people; to bind their kings with chains, and their nobles with fetters of iron; to execute upon them the judgment written: this honour have all his saints. Praise ye the Lord (Psalm 149:6–9).**

Notice the combination of God's Word and praise. They release the vengeance of the Lord and His judgments that are written throughout Scripture. He wants His vengeance and judgments released in the earth at this time. Later on, we will look at the amazing, prophetic praise that Hannah releases in 1 Samuel 2. God wants to release prophetic praise on a whole new level that will bring great change in the earth. It's actually beginning to be released now. There is no greater power than

Hannah Roars

the anointed spoken word. That is how everything was created in the beginning, and that is still God's method for bringing order out of chaos.

Passion and Persistence

In 1 Samuel 1:6 we see that her adversary provoked Hannah, to make her roar, to make her thunder. Let's move on to verse 7: *"And as he did so year by year, when she went up to the house of the Lord, so she* [Peninnah] *provoked her."* Hannah got angry, she got serious, and she got passionate. Where is the passion in the body of Christ? I believe it's coming back. We are going to receive the same passion and zeal that the Lord has.

Verses 7-8 continue: *"Therefore she wept, and did not eat. Then said Elkanah her husband to her, Hannah, why weepest thou? and why eatest thou not? and why is thy heart grieved? am not I better to thee than ten sons?"* Hannah had it fairly good. She had the love of her husband and was fully provided for, but she would not settle for *good*. She knew she had a greater destiny. She wanted God's *best*. Verses 10 and 11: *"And she was in bitterness of soul, and prayed unto the Lord, and wept sore. And she vowed a vow, and said, O Lord of hosts* [the God of armies, the God who is in control], *if thou wilt indeed look on the affliction of thine handmaid, and remember me, and not forget thine handmaid, but wilt give unto thine handmaid a man child* [this word *child* means "seed, a man seed"], *then I will give him unto the Lord all the days of his life, and there shall no razor come upon his head."* In other words, she wasn't going to touch the glory. Hair in Scripture often represents the glory. Remember, Hannah represents the barren church that is so hungry for the Lord that when she does bear fruit she will give it back to the Lord and not try to control it. That would indeed be something new. But that's exactly what will happen.

God wants to get you to a place in prayer where you press, where you push. In Matthew 11:12 Jesus stated, *"the kingdom of heaven suffereth violence, and the violent take it by force."* The word for *violence* means "to use force, to force one's way into."[11] How many of us are ready to force ourselves into the place of victory? It's time to force yourself into

---

11. Strong, *Strong's Exhaustive Concordance*, G971.

the way of being fruitful, force yourself into the way of getting your circumstances turned around. We are not talking about being forceful or aggressive that our will would come to pass; we are to be forceful and aggressive about seeing God's will come to pass. We must no longer hold back and live in complacency and mediocrity. We have been living way below God's covenant will for our lives for far too long. God has placed the ball in our court, so to speak. Let's allow adversity to provoke the Lion of the tribe of Judah to roar in us. Now is the time to rule and reign in His name.

The Name of Jesus

Before Jesus ascended back to the Father, He said that all authority had been given to Him. He then delegated that authority to His church and told us to go forth in the power of that name (see Matthew 28). It's time to rely on that name. Let's trust in the name of Jesus and use that name like never before.

Some trust in chariots, and some in horses: but we will remember the name of the Lord our God (Psalm 20:7).

He has given us power and authority to use His name. He said that whatsoever we would bind on earth would be bound in heaven. He said if we would ask or demand anything in His name He would do it. I'm not going to say as some, *Where is the God of Elijah?* I'm going to say, *He's my God. And He is in me!"* I don't have to ask where He is.

In the name of Jesus we must start demanding oppression to go. Start decreeing—sickness, you must go! Division, leave my family! Rebellion, leave my children. Confusion, depression, leave in Jesus' name! Hopelessness, leave! Barrenness, I command you in the name above all names, the name of the One with whom I am raised and seated far above all principalities, and powers, and might, and dominion (see Ephesians 1:21), leave in the name of Jesus! In the name of Jesus I speak life, I speak health, I speak vision, I speak fruitfulness—it's my time! It's the bride's time. The set time to favor Zion has come (see Psalm 102:13). I'm going to reproduce Christ in the earth. I'm being conformed into His very image (see Romans 8:29).

Hannah Roars

Importunity: The Quality of Being Shameless and Offensively Bold

And it came to pass, as she continued praying to the Lord... (1 Samuel 1:12).

Notice that Hannah continued. She did not quit or grow weary. There's something about persistence that pleases the Lord. Let's take a closer look at the parable Jesus told concerning prayer and endurance in Luke 11. Jesus went to the mountain to pray, and when He came back down His disciples wanted Him to teach them how to pray. He then instructed them to pray this way: *"Our Father which art in heaven, hallowed be thy name. Thy kingdom come. Thy will be done, as in heaven, so in earth"* (Luke 11:2). He goes on to teach them a parable regarding prayer.

Give Me Three Loaves

The parable tells of a certain man who had visitors arrive but no food for them, and it was late at night. So he went to his friend's house and asked for three loaves. Why three? Remember, two loaves speak of the Feast of Pentecost. This celebration involved two loaves of bread made with leaven. As wonderful as Pentecost is, we need to go further and deeper. We have seen revivals in the last two decades that were, quite possibly, quintessential Pentecostal revivals. People were saved and baptized in the Holy Spirit. People were healed, and there were signs, wonders, and miracles. These revivals were true moves of God, but works of the flesh and sin (leaven) were involved. Two loaves with leaven, plenty of corruption. That's Pentecost—wonderful but incomplete.

The man in the parable says, *I want three loaves*. That's going beyond Pentecost. I love Pentecost, but we have been celebrating that feast for almost two thousand years and still live in an earth that's, in many ways, more lost and wicked now than it ever was. We've come to a place where even prayer in schools is not wanted. Before they took prayer out of our schools, simply chewing gum during class was considered a major disciplinary problem. Now students are bringing weapons to school. I don't know about you, but I want three loaves. I want to go beyond Pentecost, beyond the earnest or down payment. The church must come into the fullness of her inheritance. As wonderful as the "earnest" or "down payment" of the Spirit has been (see Ephesians 1:13-14), we must long for and press for the fullness of our inheritance (see Ephesians 3:19).

Remember, in the parable the neighbor says, *I'm in bed, my children are in bed, leave me alone, friend.* Jesus said that the sleeping man will answer the door anyway, not because of friendship but because of his friend's persistent knocking—because of his importunity. Hannah had importunity. She kept praying, she kept asking. *No* was not an option. Concerning the meaning of this parable, Jesus goes on to say that anyone who continues seeking, knocking, and praying will be answered. It's about true faith and persistence.

I'm not talking about being persistent in begging, bawling, and squalling. No, I'm talking about being persistent in faith, being persistent in reminding God of His covenant promises, and being persistent in decreeing what His Word declares. It's time for the church to enter into her promised land. We will have to do what Joshua was told to do as he prepared to bring the people into their Promised Land.

> **This book of the law shall not depart out of thy mouth; but thou shalt meditate therein day and night, that thou mayest observe to do according to all that is written therein: for then thou shalt make thy way prosperous, and then thou shalt have good success (Joshua 1:8).**

The Anointed Spoken Word

Most Christians today let days go by without speaking God's Word. We need to come up to God's way of doing things, and His way involves using the spoken Word. We need to value the power and effectiveness of the *anointed spoken word*. Imagine if decrees and praises from God's Word were continually on our lips. Are you performing your end of the covenant?

> **As for me, this is my covenant with them, saith the Lord; My spirit that is upon thee, and my words which I have put in thy mouth, shall not depart out of thy mouth, nor out of the**

mouth of thy seed, nor out of the mouth of thy seed's seed, saith the Lord, from henceforth and for ever (Isaiah 59:21).

Thou shalt also decree a thing, and it shall be established unto thee: and the light shall shine upon thy ways (Job 22:28).

We are commanded in the Scriptures to not only believe God's promises but to speak them forth and remind Him of them.

Put me in remembrance: let us plead together: declare thou, that thou mayest be justified (Isaiah 43:26).

Imagine the acceleration and advancement of the kingdom of God in our lives and in the earth if His Word were continually on our lips.

Then said the Lord unto me, Thou hast well seen: for I will hasten my word to perform it (Jeremiah 1:12).

Angels are released as we speak the Word. Remember, we are His body. We are His voice in the earth.

Bless the Lord, ye his angels, that excel in strength, that do his commandments, hearkening unto the voice of his word (Psalm 103:20).

David was a foreshadow of Christ. He was successful in subduing the enemies of God's people, and he turned the kingdom over to his son, Solomon, in relative peace. David knew the secret of releasing the anointed spoken Word. David's last words on earth showed that he greatly understood the importance and power of releasing the anointed spoken Word.

Now these be the last words of David. David the son of Jesse said, and the man who was raised up on high, the anointed of the God of Jacob, and the sweet psalmist of Israel, said, The Spirit of the Lord spake by me, and his word was in my tongue (2 Samuel 23:1-2).

Wow! May that be our testimony as well—that the Spirit of the Lord speaks through us and that His Word is on our tongue. It's time to be doers of the Word. Let's come out of deception, humble ourselves and

HANNAH ROARS

admit that we have not been doing this as we should. Let's ask for God's grace. He will not withhold it from those who admit their need and ask for it.

> **Wherefore lay apart all filthiness and superfluity of naughtiness, and receive with meekness the engrafted word, which is able to save your souls. But be ye doers of the word, and not hearers only, deceiving your own selves (James 1:21-22).**

It's time to shift gears in prayer. It's time to go from begging to decreeing. Yes, there are some things to ask for, but there are other things that He has already declared to be ours. Instead of begging God to bless you or heal you, why not come into agreement with His Word that your victory has already been provided through the atonement? Why not boldly declare, *I'm the healed of the Lord. Father, I thank You that my days of suffering with this sickness are over. I am the blessed of the Lord. Your Word says that You took my infirmities and bore my sicknesses and by Your stripes I was healed* (see Matthew 8:17 and 1 Peter 2:24). Persist in these declarations.

Shamelessly Bold

The word *importunity*[12] used in Jesus' parable in Luke 11 means "shamelessness, impudence (the quality of being offensively bold)." Are you ready to walk in this type of faith—one in which you appear offensively bold? I'm talking about the type of boldness that Charles Finney and Father Daniel Nash walked in; at times it scared even them. Charles Finney and Father Daniel Nash were itinerant ministers in the Northeast United States and led revival meetings in the 1820s and 1830s. Father Nash usually arrived in a town two weeks before Finney and locked himself in a room and prayed until Finney got there. Together they were used mightily of God; many people came to know the Lord during this time which came to be known as the Second Great Awakening. Finney would get into such a powerful prayer flow, such a roar, that he would hear himself say things like, "Father, don't think

---

12. Geoffrey William Bromiley, *The International Standard Bible Encyclopedia* (Grand Rapids, MI: W.B. Eerdmans, 1979), s.v. "importunity."

Hannah Roars

I came to this city and we're not having revival. We are going to have revival here! Your Word promises that if I preach the gospel, signs and wonders will follow and people will get saved!" Finney was often shocked at his own boldness in prayer. But he knew it was inspired of God and was coming up from his spirit man. The enemy often comes to quench such boldness with condemning thoughts such as, *Who do you think you are? You're not worthy. You had a fight with your wife this week. You kicked the dog. You didn't read enough Scripture,* etc. We must rise up and declare the truth: *I have boldness by the blood of Jesus* (see Hebrews 10:19). *I put no confidence in me but I put all confidence in God and what He did at the cross, and His Word says I can come* **boldly** *to the throne of grace through the blood of Jesus.*

Are you ready to go to another realm where you are effective in prayer but potentially offensive to people, especially religious people? You won't offend God with your boldness but you will offend religious people. Religious people often mistake boldness for pride. But false humility, which is often exhibited by the religious crowd, is actually one of the worst forms of pride. The Lord told me that His fire and His boldness are about to come upon His people like never before and many religious people will be offended. Are you ready to be bold?

The Lord Is Coming Out!

This new level of boldness, importunity, and authority in prayer is actually the Lord Himself rising up within His people. The Lord is arising within His church, which is His temple and habitation in the earth.

> **Be silent, O all flesh, before the Lord: for he is raised up out of his holy habitation (Zechariah 2:13).**

Not only is the Lord now arising within His people, but He is also going to come out or flow out of us in a way that will bring change to everything.

> **For, behold, the Lord cometh out of his place to punish the inhabitants of the earth for their iniquity: the earth also**

shall disclose her blood, and shall no more cover her slain (Isaiah 26:21).

Did you hear that? The earth will disclose her blood. The injustices will be uncovered and avenged. All things are about to be turned right-side-up. As we will soon discuss, Hannah prophesied all things would be overturned. We need to fervently pray and decree the above-mentioned Scriptures in Zechariah and Isaiah and many more like them. I will include a list of such Scriptures at the end of this book that you can decree. The Word declares we are to remind God of His Word in order to see His will done in the earth.

Avenge Me of My Adversary

Remember the parable that Jesus told in Luke 18 that men ought always to pray and faint not? There was a widow who went before the judge and said *avenge me of my adversary*. Are you ready to see the innocent avenged of their adversary? It's time to rise up and roar against the adversity that the enemy sent to destroy us. It's time to see the Lord's vengeance as promised in Luke 18:7: *"and shall not God avenge His own elect, which cry day and night unto Him."* No matter what state of barrenness you may be experiencing, now is definitely not the time to give up! Verse 7 continues: *"and shall not God avenge His own elect, which cry day and night unto Him, though he bear long with them?"* I don't necessarily like that last phrase, *"though He bear long with them."* It implies that God is going to let you go on for a bit without an immediate answer to see if you really believe. I'm tired of microwave Christians who believe God for a short period of time and then give up. The next verse adds some encouragement: *"I tell you that He will avenge them speedily"* (Luke 18:8). In context, by the term *speedily*, He means not necessarily immediately, but quickly. Remember, it's through faith and endurance that we inherit the promises (see Hebrews 6:12). The verse continues with a sober question: *"Nevertheless when the Son of man cometh, shall he find faith on the earth?"* (Luke 18:8). As Jesus admonished, we must pray without fainting or giving up.

Break up your fallow ground: for it is time to seek the Lord, till he come and rain righteousness upon you (Hosea 10:12).

Hannah Roars

A new grace is coming upon God's people to fervently pray and seek the Lord "*till he rains righteousness upon us.*" That means until everything is made right. Things are not right in the earth at this time but the mountains will soon be made low and the valleys exalted. The overturning of all things is upon us! Don't stop praying and seeking the Lord until His will is done on earth as it is in heaven. This is not a pipe dream; it is the Word of God.

Chapter 6: The Roar of the Lord

Chapter 6
The Roar of the Lord

We must remember that it is the zeal of the Lord that advances His kingdom (see Isaiah 9:7). It is His grace which will allow us to overcome the complacency and indifference that is so prevalent in this Laodicean church era. The roar that is arising within the Lord's remnant today is actually the Lord Himself roaring!

The Lord shall go forth as a mighty man, he shall stir up jealousy like a man of war: he shall cry, yea, roar; he shall prevail against his enemies (Isaiah 42:13).

The Lord is called the Lion of Judah, and He lives in us and prevails in us.

And one of the elders saith unto me, Weep not: behold, the Lion of the tribe of Judah, the Root of David, hath prevailed to open the book, and to loose the seven seals thereof (Revelation 5:5).

He not only lives in us, but He is actively at work within us.

For it is God which worketh in you both to will and to do of his good pleasure (Philippians 2:13).

The Lord is indeed beginning to release His roar, but we must remain aware of the fact that He is releasing His roar in and through us, His church, His body.

Therefore prophesy thou against them all these words, and say unto them, The Lord shall roar from on high, and utter

his voice from his holy habitation; he shall mightily roar upon his habitation; he shall give a shout, as they that tread the grapes, against all the inhabitants of the earth (Jeremiah 25:30).

Notice that the Lord roars and utters His voice from His habitation—that's us. Notice also that His roar will have an effect on His people, as well as on all the inhabitants of the earth.

The Bible has been likened to the title of Charles Dickens' famous book, *A Tale of Two Cities,* because from Genesis to Revelation we read about the two cities of Jerusalem and Babylon. We know from many Scriptures, including Hebrews 12 and Revelation 21, that Jerusalem is representative of His bride. A thorough study of the scriptural references to Babylon will reveal that Babylon is representative of those who are not the Lord's, but are indeed *of the world.* Babylon can include the current worldly political, economic, and educational systems that are so vehemently opposed to biblical precepts. My point is not to define Babylon, but to confirm Babylon's part in causing the shaking of the world's kingdoms.

The Lord also shall roar out of Zion, and utter his voice from Jerusalem; and the heavens and the earth shall shake: but the Lord will be the hope of his people, and the strength of the children of Israel (Joel 3:16).

Again, it is the Lord roaring out of His people, out of Zion, that brings the shaking to the earth and strength and deliverance to His people. As Philippians 2:13 states, it is the Lord who is at work within us that accomplishes His purposes.

Great Focus

The Lord will not force His will or His working within us. We must learn to cooperate with Him and flow with Him. We must learn to allow Him to roar in us. In this era of complacency and endless distractions, this will take great focus and determination. Few people throughout history have learned the secret of allowing God to be released in and through them in a significant way. But those who did were world changers. God

The Roar of the Lord

is preparing to release a company of world changers. Many Samuels will be birthed in this hour who will bring change to everything.

Notice that as the *roar of the Lord* is released, great change is released upon the earth and its kingdoms (mountains) and all of God's enemies are dealt with.

> **The Lord shall go forth as a mighty man, he shall stir up jealousy like a man of war: he shall cry, yea, roar; he shall prevail against his enemies. I have long time holden my peace; I have been still, and refrained myself: now will I cry like a travailing woman; I will destroy and devour at once. I will make waste mountains and hills (Isaiah 42:13–15).**

Notice how it says that God has been holding His peace and restraining Himself until now, but now He will go forth as a mighty man of war and as a travailing (birthing) woman. God is about to unveil Himself and will be seen in a way that many have never seen Him before. Many have not understood the zealous nature of the Lord and have assumed Him to be indifferent concerning the affairs of men. But this is not so. The earth is about to see Him as He really is.

Roaring Fires

> **The Lord is not slack concerning his promise, as some men count slackness; but is longsuffering to us-ward, not willing that any should perish, but that all should come to repentance. But the day of the Lord will come as a thief in the night; in the which the heavens shall pass away with a great noise, and the elements shall melt with fervent heat, the earth also and the works that are therein shall be burned up (2 Peter 3:9-10).**

It is interesting to note that the word *elements* in the above verse does not refer to the physical atomic elements from the periodic table of elements from which the physical universe is made. The word *elements* in this verse is the Greek word *stoicheion* which means "orderly arrangement."[13] If you look at the other times this word is used in the

---

13. Strong, *Strong's Exhaustive Concordance*, G4747.

HANNAH ROARS

New Testament, it becomes clear that *elements* has nothing to do with the physical elements melting. It actually refers to the melting of the orderly arrangement and principles of this current world system. In fact this same word *elements,* in other New Testament passages, is more accurately translated as rudiments or principles. The principles and rudiments of this world system, which have been under the power of the wicked one, are about to be completely transformed. That is what is being released today.

Keep in mind that God is a Spirit and He is described in Scripture as *"a consuming fire"* (Hebrews 12:29). Because God is a spirit, this is not a physical fire we are discussing here, but a spiritual fire. The whole world is about to experience this fire's heat. This is what is being birthed today in and through God's Hannahs. The book of Malachi describes in detail the day we are entering into.

> **Behold, I will send my messenger, and he shall prepare the way before me: and the Lord, whom ye seek, shall suddenly come to his temple, even the messenger of the covenant, whom ye delight in: behold, he shall come, saith the Lord of hosts. But who may abide the day of his coming? and who shall stand when he appeareth? for he is like a refiners fire, and like fullers' soap: and he shall sit as a refiner and purifier of silver: and he shall purify the sons of Levi, and purge them as gold and silver (Malachi 3:1–3).**

Both Malachi and Hannah prophesied of the overturning of the kingdoms of the prideful and the exaltation of His people. And it shall be the fire of God that accomplishes this. Look at the next chapter in Malachi.

> **For, behold, the day cometh, that shall burn as an oven; and all the proud, yea, and all that do wickedly, shall be stubble: and the day that cometh shall burn them up, saith the Lord of hosts, that it shall leave them neither root nor branch. But unto you that fear my name shall the Sun of righteousness arise with healing in his wings; and ye shall go forth, and grow up as calves of the stall. And ye shall tread down the wicked; for they shall be ashes under the**

The Roar of the Lord

soles of your feet in the day that I shall do this, saith the Lord of hosts (Malachi 4:1–3).

Remember that God is a spirit and this fire and heat are spiritual in essence. Spiritual things are much more real, powerful, and effective than physical things. And the efficacy of God's fire is infinitely greater than any natural fire that man can produce, including the fire and heat released through nuclear weapons.

Messengers of Fire

Not only is God described as a fire, but so are His messengers.

Who maketh his angels spirits; his ministers a flaming fire (Psalm 104:4).

The people of God have always been called to be a fire that consumes, so to speak, the enemies of God.

And the house of Jacob shall be a fire, and the house of Joseph a flame, and the house of Esau for stubble, and they shall kindle in them, and devour them; and there shall not be any remaining of the house of Esau; for the Lord hath spoken it (Obadiah 1:18).

The roaring fires of God are actually released through His bond servants. The fire that is released through them is not a literal fire but fire that is spiritual in nature. This fire that His people are to release is inherently contained in the Word of God.

Is not my word like as a fire? saith the Lord; and like a hammer that breaketh the rock in pieces? (Jeremiah 23:29)

Many Christians who teach and preach God's Word make it seem to be more like a feather than a fire or a hammer. We live in a day when many Christian leaders are going to great lengths to make sure God's Word appears to be completely non-offensive and politically correct. But as God's people become the fiery ministers they are called to be, cleansing and refinement will be brought to the church and then to the world. An unprecedented fiery anointing is about to be released through the people of God as they speak forth His Word. This will result in the same type of power that was released in Genesis 1:2-3. God spoke life, light, and order to the earth when it was *"without form, and void; and darkness was upon the face of the deep"* (Genesis 1:2).

The Two Witnesses

The fact that the fire of God is released through His people is seen throughout Scripture. One of my favorite places that speaks of this fire is Revelation 11, concerning the Two Witnesses.

> **And I will give power unto my two witnesses, and they shall prophesy a thousand two hundred and threescore days, clothed in sackcloth. These are the two olive trees, and the two candlesticks standing before the God of the earth (Revelation 11:3-4).**

Notice that the Bible declares exactly who these two witnesses are. We do not have to guess. The Bible (not me), says in verse 4 that these are the two olive trees and the two candlesticks. This is a direct reference to Zechariah 4, which is about God's temple, His house (remember, that's you) being rebuilt against all opposition. In Zechariah 4 we see that this temple will be built but not by man's might or power, but by God's Spirit, by His anointing. This is a message that the church really needs to hear in this hour when the methods of man are being embraced by many.

We must interpret Scripture with Scripture and not try to figure out the Bible with our carnal minds. The Bible states in Revelation 11:4 that the two witnesses are the two candlesticks, and Revelation 1:20 states that the candlesticks are a direct reference to the church.

> **The seven candlesticks which thou sawest are the seven churches (Revelation 1:20).**

There were seven candlesticks (churches) in the book of Revelation but only two of them seemed to be fully obeying the Lord to the degree that He did not find any defilement or fault in them. Prophecy can be multifaceted but certainly *the two witnesses can represent God's obedient church.*

The Roar of the Lord

Now notice what is proceeding out of the mouth of His two witnesses (His obedient church, His bondservants)—fire!

And if any man will hurt them, fire proceedeth out of their mouth, and devoureth their enemies: and if any man will hurt them, he must in this manner be killed (Revelation 11:5).

While watching a popular, end-time, Christian movie that supposedly contained scenes from the book of Revelation, I grievously and yet comically observed that the producers portrayed the two witnesses as two literal men. These men shot literal fire out of their mouths that burned people to death. Mature Christians would never desire the power to have literal fire come out of their mouths to kill their enemies and make them look like marshmallows that were placed a little too close to a campfire! Friends, the only fire that God wants coming out of the mouths of His people is the fire of His Word, which is far more powerful and effective in cleansing the earth and devouring His enemies than a literal fire.

These have power to shut heaven, that it rain not in the days of their prophecy: and have power over waters to turn them to blood, and to smite the earth with all plagues, as often as they will (Revelation 11:6).

Of course, the power to shut the heaven that it rains not, to turn the waters into blood, and smite the earth with plagues, are direct references to the ministries of Elijah and Moses. Yes, powerful anointings like those which Moses and Elijah walked in, and greater, will be seen in the earth once again. These anointings are to release God's judgments, both in the church and in the world. Moses was used to bring deliverance to God's people and to bring great judgment upon Egypt and its pharaoh. Egypt is a type of the world and pharaoh is a type of the devil. Elijah was anointed to bring corrective judgments and chastening to Israel. Israel is a type of the people of God.

Tremendous Power through Energized Prayer

Let's not underestimate the transforming power that will be released through the anointed, fervent prayers of God's people. The Amplified Bible reads like this:

HANNAH ROARS

The earnest (heartfelt, continued) **prayer of a righteous man makes tremendous power available (James 5:16 AMP).**

The word *earnest* in verse 16 is the Greek word *energeo* from which we get the word *energy* or *energized*.[14] The Lord is about to energize our prayer life and roar through us in such a way that will make tremendous power available! However, we must be willing to pay the price and put the distractions of this world and the things of the flesh aside to seek Him as never before.

God is a rewarder of those who diligently seek Him. Our energized prayers will break the powers of darkness and release the glory and promises of God. But we are going to have to learn to release God's thunder and God's roar. We have to learn to labor in the Spirit and give birth to the things God wants released in this hour. God wants Hannahs who will pray and not faint until righteousness is rained upon us. Let's pray and see Samuel birthed. *Samuel* means "that which was asked for" (see 1 Samuel 1:20). Don't give up until that which you've asked for is birthed. We're asking for the Jesus ministry. We want the three loaves. We want to go beyond Pentecost, the first fruits of our inheritance, into the tabernacles ministry, the fullness of our inheritance; and we're not going to give up. Some may want to just play church, but God is raising up an army. He's raising up Hannahs. They might look pretty lowly right now and appear to be in a state of barrenness, but just wait. Everything is about to change!

Mockery and False Judgment Silenced

And it came to pass, as she continued praying before the Lord, that Eli marked her mouth. Now Hannah, she spake in her heart; only her lips moved, but her voice was not heard: therefore Eli thought she had been drunken (1 Samuel 1:12-13).

This was a woman who was fervent and passionate in her prayer. She wasn't just casually praying something like this: *Dear Father, I just ask Your blessing upon me.* It was more like: *Dear God, I'm not going to be satisfied until barrenness is completely removed from my life!*

---

14. Strong, *Strong's Exhaustive Concordance*, G1754.

The Roar of the Lord

Barrenness is not a part of the covenant, so I won't stand for it. I will have fruit in my life. And what I produce will not be common. It will be extraordinary. It will be something new and different that will bring much needed change. She was praying and acting so beside herself that Eli thought she was drunk. She wasn't drunk. She was lost in prayer. Her lips moved. The roar has nothing to do with physical loudness or strength. People can be loud or strong but be completely in the flesh and release no spiritual power. The weapons of our warfare are not carnal (physical or fleshly) but are mighty through God. The key is that she spoke from her heart, her spirit.

Charles Finney, who was used by God to birth great revival and awakening in his day, called it being given over to "a spirit of prayer." Evan Roberts, who was used to help birth the Welsh Revival that impacted the entire globe, was so given over to desperate prayer, that he was greatly criticized by most Christians and was even accused of being somewhat mentally ill. The average Christian, like Eli, will not understand the hunger and desperation of the Hannahs who are now arising in the earth. Many in Christendom and religious Babylon are already wondering what is wrong with those who have caught a glimpse of the high calling and are pressing for it. I pray that the Lord will find that type of hunger and determination in us. I don't think we are quite there yet. But He is drawing us.

Groaning and Travailing

Did you ever get so desperate in prayer that you could barely speak? It is the Spirit of God Himself groaning and travailing in us. God is birthing something extraordinary and unprecedented through His bride. It's the roar of the Lord in and through us. It will be extremely effective and thorough in bringing great and needed change.

> **Likewise the Spirit also helpeth our infirmities: for we know not what we should pray for as we ought: but the Spirit itself maketh intercession for us with groanings which cannot be uttered (Romans 8:26).**

HANNAH ROARS

God Has Not Given Us a Spirit of Timidity

Don't cower back or give in to the mockery and intimidation that is often released by religious spirits against true disciples of Christ. We live in an hour when many are crying *sensationalism* at anything that has to do with the high calling of God. We must keep our eyes on Him and not allow anything or anyone to distract us.

And Eli said unto her, How long wilt thou be drunken? put away thy wine from thee. And Hannah answered and said, No, my lord, I am a woman of a sorrowful spirit (1 Samuel 1:14-15).

That word translated *sorrowful* actually means "fierce, severe, hard, cruel, stiff-necked, and rigorous."[15] God's new breed is indeed a stubborn, obstinate group of people—not obstinate toward God or His laws but obstinate toward things in their lives that are contrary to Him and His covenant. You will be mocked by religion. When I look at some of the firstfruits company of people who have been used greatly by God, I can see their stubborn, stiff-necked, harsh, intense spirit. God has always had a people with the attitude: *I'm not drunk; I'm not out of my mind. I believe God's Word. I will have and experience what His Word says even if no one else ever has. If His Word says it, I believe it, and that settles it. I'm bringing my experience up to the level of God's Word and not vice versa. I won't take barrenness anymore. I won't give up until I see God's purposes birthed in the earth.* I am not saying we are to be ambitious. However, we must have something in our spirit man that will not allow us to simply read "by Jesus' stripes we are healed" and not walk in it (see 1 Peter 2:24). Or, "my God meets all my needs" and not walk in it (see Philippians 4:19). Or, "we can rule and reign in life" and not walk in it (see Romans 5:17). Or, *"the works that I do shall he do also, and greater works"* and not walk in it (John 14:12). Even now, God is raising up a people who are saying: *If God's Word says it, then I'm going to walk in it.* These are modern-day Hannahs who have the tenacity of a bulldog. They will hold on to God's covenant

---

15. Strong, *Strong's Exhaustive Concordance*, H7186.

The Roar of the Lord

promises and never let them go. It's time for God's fierce, dread champions to arise.

Shalom

> **I have drunk neither wine nor strong drink, but have poured out my soul before the Lord. Count not thine handmaid for a daughter of Belial** [the devil, worthlessness]**: for out of the abundance of my complaint and grief have I spoken hitherto. Then Eli answered and said, Go in peace (1 Samuel 1:15–17).**

He said, "Shalom, woman, you are now whole." Don't think God didn't speak through Eli. Even when Samuel was raised up and prophesied the death of Eli's sons, Eli said *"It is the Lord: let him do what seemeth him good"* (1 Samuel 3:18). Eli knew he was weak and spineless, but he was still God's priest. Eli spoke the Word of the Lord—*go in peace*. Peace is the Hebrew word *shalom.* Shalom means *wholeness, soundness.*[16]

> **And the God of Israel grant thee thy petition that thou hast asked of Him. And she said, Let thine handmaid find grace in thy sight (1 Samuel 1:17-18).**

There is a grace that is coming to the people of God. There is an ability that is coming from God to do what we haven't been able to do.

> **So the woman went her way, and did eat, and her countenance was no more sad. And they rose up in the morning early, and worshipped before the Lord** [praise is a key]**, and returned, and came to their house to Ramah: and Elkanah knew Hannah his wife; and the Lord remembered her (1 Samuel 1:18-19).**

The One who allowed her womb to be shut is the One who also brought out of her this fierceness, this queenlike dominion.

---

16. Strong, *Strong's Exhaustive Concordance*, H7965.

HANNAH ROARS

The High Calling

> **Wherefore it came to pass, when the time was come about after Hannah had conceived, that she bare a son, and called his name Samuel, saying, Because I have asked him of the Lord (1 Samuel 1:20).**

There is something truly amazing coming to the body of Christ, and those who have asked for it will walk in it. There are some blessings that we may have simply stumbled into in the past; but the *high calling* is not one of them. As Paul stated, it must be *pressed* into.

> **This one thing I do, forgetting those things which are behind, and reaching forth unto those things which are before, I press toward the mark for the prize of the high calling of God in Christ Jesus (Philippians 3:13-14).**

In the very next verse, Paul goes on to state that every mature Christian should have this same mindset.

> **Let us therefore, as many as be perfect, be thus minded (Philippians 3:15).**

How many Christians do you know who are even aware of the high calling or are pressing into it? Remember, it is Samuel who helped usher in David and the Davidic kingdom, which is a type of Christ and His kingdom. Samuel didn't come easily, and that which God is birthing will not haphazardly fall into our laps. It will be His instrument that will usher in the kingdom of God. It will come to people who choose to focus beyond the cares of this life and worldly distractions, a people who seek the Lord and His kingdom—first.

> **And the man Elkanah, and all his house, went up to offer unto the Lord the yearly sacrifice, and his vow. But Hannah went not up; for she said unto her husband, I will not go up until the child be weaned, and then I will bring him, that he may appear before the Lord, and there abide forever. And Elkanah her husband said unto her, Do what seemeth thee good; tarry until thou have weaned him; only the Lord establish his word (1 Samuel 1:21–23).**

The Roar of the Lord

The Lord is establishing, making firm, His Word. It's not simply the truth you know that builds strength; it is the truth that you walk in. God is taking us from knowing truth in our heads to actually knowing truth in our hearts and walking in that truth. It is what you walk in that you really believe. Faith without works (corresponding action) isn't really faith at all. James 1:22 tells us that we are deceived if we only hear God's Word but don't do His Word. Obviously, that leaves all of us, to some degree, in a state of deception. But thankfully, God, in His mercy and grace, is finishing the work that He has begun in us. The Lord is establishing His Word.

> **So the woman abode, and gave her son suck until she weaned him. And when she had weaned him, she took him up with her, with three bullocks, and one ephah of flour and a bottle of wine, and brought him unto the house of the Lord in Shiloh: and the child was young. And they slew a bullock, and brought the child to Eli. And she said, Oh my lord, as thy soul liveth, my lord, I am the woman that stood by thee here, praying unto the Lord. For this child I prayed; and the Lord hath given me my petition which I asked of Him (1 Samuel 1:23–27).**

Are you ready to see the fulfillment of God's covenant promises in your life and in the earth? The Peninnahs may have mocked us, barely tolerated us, and rolled their eyes at us saying, *Yeah, right, the Jesus ministry? The high calling? That's sensationalism.* All of God's Word will be fulfilled. Jesus will have a people who are conformed to His image and who walk in His character and display His power.

> **Therefore also I have lent him to the Lord; as long as he liveth he shall be lent to the Lord (1 Samuel 1:28).**

Hannah completely gave back to the Lord that which was birthed through her. So it will be with the glorious thing that God is birthing through His bride. We will not try to control or lay claim to it. We will indeed lay our crowns at His feet.

Chapter 7: Hannah's Prophecy

Chapter 7
Hannah's Prophecy

First Samuel 2:1 goes on to tell the rest of the story: *"And Hannah prayed."* This so-called prayer of Hannah's didn't consist of one petition but was actually a progression of praises, prophetic decrees, *and* prophecy. Hannah, like David, knew how to employ the combination of the high praises of God and the two-edged sword of the Word, which always results in the release of God's righteous judgments in the earth (see Psalm 149:6-9). Here is her prayer/prophecy:

> **And Hannah prayed, and said, My heart rejoiceth in the Lord, mine horn is exalted in the Lord: my mouth is enlarged over mine enemies; because I rejoice in thy salvation. There is none holy as the Lord: for there is none beside thee: neither is there any rock like our God (1 Samuel 2:1-2).**

She released a powerful, prophetic praise and began to prophesy about this end-time ministry that is going to turn everything around. This prophecy actually has next to nothing to do with Samuel. It has to do with you and the turn around that is upon us. The Lord is about to turn the tables over again. The Peninnahs are about to be brought down and the Hannahs are going to be exalted. We are coming to a day where Christendom (dead religion and religiosity) is coming down and godless people in places of authority are all about to be displaced. The Hannahs are arising and they are birthing a brand-new breed of Christians in the earth. What is actually being birthed is true Christianity—Christians who are completely conformed to the image of Christ.

HANNAH ROARS

Unprecedented Trouble

Don't grow weary as you watch those around you, even those in Christendom, produce child after child while you appear barren. Perhaps God in His divine wisdom and foresight has allowed or even orchestrated your barrenness so that you will press into His presence. As a result, you will become one of His most intimate friends who is so united with Him that He is able to produce something truly extraordinary in and through you. The principle remains true: the greater the call, the more difficult the struggle. Anything that comes too easily is generally not very significant; and what God is bringing forth in this hour is extremely significant. You have been chosen to live in a time of some of the greatest trouble and shaking that has ever been seen on the earth.

And at that time shall Michael stand up, the great prince which standeth for the children of thy people: and there shall be a time of trouble, such as never was since there was a nation even to that same time: and at that time thy people shall be delivered, every one that shall be found written in the book (Daniel 12:1).

I'm sure all the other non-barren women in Hannah's day were producing many good children, but Hannah would go on to produce something truly amazing—Samuel. It was Samuel who would speak to the corruption in the priesthood and utterly deal with King Agag and the Amalekites (a type of the flesh). It was Samuel who literally tore the monarchy from King Saul and eventually ushered in the Davidic kingdom. God is producing His passionate church in this hour, and they will certainly be used to usher in His kingdom.

That I Might Know Him

The Lord tells us in Jeremiah 29:13: *"And ye shall seek me, and find me, when ye shall search for me with all your heart."* It is the church's intimacy with Him that will produce His Son, His Man-child. God is love and love gives. History has declared that God has truly given us His best and continues to give His all for us. I have often asked the Lord if He does anything for Himself. Ephesians 5:25-32 is one of the many passages in Scripture that declares that He has given and continues to give His all for us, His bride. He will now have a people who reciprocate that love; that people will be His bride, His church. Many people have taught about what Jesus accomplished for us through His death. We cannot overstate what His death accomplished; but we will now begin to discover and experience what He is doing through His life.

> **For if, when we were enemies, we were reconciled to God by the death of his Son, much more, being reconciled, we shall be saved by his life (Romans 5:10).**

Remember, 1 Peter 1:5 talks about a "*salvation*" coming to those who are already saved. And so does Paul in the book of Romans.

> **And that, knowing the time, that now it is high time to awake out of sleep: for now is our salvation nearer than when we believed (Romans 13:11).**

Revelation 12: This Is a "Daddy's Boy"

> **And there appeared a great wonder in heaven; a woman clothed with the sun, and the moon under her feet, and upon her head a crown of twelve stars: and she being with child cried, travailing in birth, and pained to be delivered. …And she brought forth a man child, who was to rule all nations with a rod of iron: and her child was caught up unto God, and to his throne (Revelation 12:1-2, 5).**

Christ's true church will become like the woman in Revelation 12 who is clothed with the sun (His glory and life) and who has the moon (the coldness of dead religion) under her feet. Notice that the woman in Revelation 12 does not control the man-child she just delivered, but the child was immediately caught up to God's throne. This too signifies that the glorious thing that the Lord is birthing through us will be completely given back to Him. In fact, not only will we not control it, but we will come to the place of maturity and wisdom where we will not *want* to control it. Nevertheless, the Lord does need His body, His bride, His church, to birth His purposes. But the focus is not the church; the focus is Christ. It is time to draw nearer to Him than ever before. The entire birthing process (conception, gestation, and delivery) will require

HANNAH ROARS

intimacy with the Lord. It's time to abandon ourselves in Him. It will become increasingly easy to distinguish those who are truly living for Him from those who are not.

Hannah Prophesies the Overturning of All Things

Remember, Hannah's so-called prayer contained no requests, but was a progression of praises, prophetic decrees, and prophecy. She actually prophesied the overturning of the world's kingdoms and the establishment of the kingdom of heaven on earth. The Lord was indeed roaring and thundering through her mightily. The powers of those anointed, spoken words are still mightily at work, accomplishing God's purposes. Listen to the commanding power of the Word of the Lord in the mouth of His saint.

> **Talk no more so exceeding proudly; let not arrogancy come out of your mouth: for the Lord is a God of knowledge, and by him actions are weighed. The bows of the mighty men are broken, and they that stumbled are girded with strength. They that were full have hired out themselves for bread; and they that were hungry ceased: so that the barren hath born seven; and she that hath many children is waxed feeble. The Lord killeth, and maketh alive: he bringeth down to the grave, and bringeth up. The Lord maketh poor, and maketh rich: he bringeth low, and lifteth up. He raiseth up the poor out of the dust, and lifteth up the beggar from the dunghill, to set them among princes, and to make them inherit the throne of glory: for the pillars of the earth are the Lord's, and he hath set the world upon them. He will keep the feet of his saints, and the wicked shall be silent in darkness; for by strength shall no man prevail. The adversaries of the Lord shall be broken to pieces; out of heaven shall he thunder upon them: the Lord shall judge the ends of the earth; and he shall give strength unto his king, and exalt the horn of his anointed (1 Samuel 2:3–10).**

Hannah's Prophecy

"Overturn" Times Three

Ezekiel also prophesied the overturning of the world's kingdoms and the establishment of the kingdom of God on earth. He prophesied of the removal of the diadem (the headpiece of the high priest) and the removal of the crown. This speaks of the changing of the guard in present religious and political domains. Similar to Hannah, Ezekiel also prophesied of things not being the same and of the exaltation of the humble and the abasement of the proud.

Thus saith the Lord God; Remove the diadem, and take off the crown: this shall not be the same: exalt him that is low, and abase him that is high. I will overturn, overturn, overturn, it: and it shall be no more, until he come whose right it is; and I will give it him (Ezekiel 21:26-27).

He *"whose right it is,"* is obviously and ultimately a reference to the Lord Jesus Christ. Notice that the word *overturn* is used three times in a row. It is very rare in Scripture to see a word used three times in a row. In fact, the only other places I know of in Scripture where this is done are in Isaiah 6:3, *"Holy, Holy, Holy, is the Lord of Hosts,"* and *"Holy, Holy, Holy, Lord God Almighty"* found in Revelation 4:8. Also, *"O earth, earth, earth, hear the word of the Lord"* is found in Jeremiah 22:29.

At a Jesus festival in the late 1970s, I learned from a teacher who appeared to know quite a bit about the Hebrew language that when a word was used three times in a row, it was of utmost importance and infinite significance. Of course, the holiness of God is known to be of utmost importance in knowing God and His nature; but do you realize the importance in the heart of God for the overturning that is coming? This implies that God is extremely passionate and zealous concerning the overturning of the kingdoms of the world and the establishment of His kingdom on the earth. We need to be much more like Him in our passion and zeal. Let's put on the mind of Christ. Christendom has painted a very different, or at the very least, an incomplete image of God, but He is about to reveal His full nature. He is a God of great passion and zeal.

The Lord shall go forth as a mighty man, he shall stir up jealousy like a man of war: he shall cry, yea, roar; he shall

prevail against his enemies. I have long time holden my peace; I have been still, and refrained myself: now will I cry like a travailing woman; I will destroy and devour at once. I will make waste mountains and hills, and dry up all their herbs; and I will make the rivers islands, and I will dry up the pools (Isaiah 42:13–15).

Take a look at the clothing the Lord is putting on. This will result in the *"fear of the Lord"*—which is so blatantly lacking and desperately needed—returning to the entire earth.

For he put on righteousness as a breastplate, and an helmet of salvation upon his head; and he put on the garments of vengeance for clothing, and was clad with zeal as a cloak. According to their deeds, accordingly he will repay, fury to his adversaries, recompence to his enemies; to the islands he will repay recompence. So shall they fear the name of the Lord from the west, and his glory from the rising of the sun. When the enemy shall come in like a flood, the Spirit of the Lord shall lift up a standard against him (Isaiah 59:17–19).

Isaiah 64 tells us that the Lord will manifest His presence in such a way that the kingdoms of this world will melt or flow down at His presence. He is about to make His name (His true nature) known to His adversaries and nations will tremble at His presence. It will not be business as usual in this hour.

Oh that thou wouldest rend the heavens, that thou wouldest come down, that the mountains might flow down at thy presence, as when the melting fire burneth, the fire causeth the waters to boil, to make thy name known to thine adversaries, that the nations may tremble at thy presence! (Isaiah 64:1-2)

The Noise of Many Waters

It would be of great benefit to prayerfully study Hannah's entire prophecy. It is coming to pass swiftly in our day, and we have a leading role to play. God wants to fill our mouths with this same type of anointed, prophetic prayer to see His desires come to fruition. Hannah's anointed

Hannah's Prophecy

prophetic word is still powerfully at work in the earth today. As more and more of the members of His body learn to release this type of anointed, prophetic prayer, the intervention and power of God being released in the earth will increase exponentially.

His roar will be heard and it will sound like "the noise of many waters" because the rivers will be flowing through His many-membered body. As we step up to the plate, His roar and thunder will be irresistibly heard like never before. Then the earth will see the brightness of His glory.

And, behold, the glory of the God of Israel came from the way of the east: and his voice was like a noise of many waters: and the earth shined with his glory (Ezekiel 43:2).

Chapter 8: Roaring Rivers

Chapter 8
Roaring Rivers

The Pouring Out of the Water

Jesus spoke of these rivers being released when He performed one of His most significant prophetic acts of His three-and-a-half-year earthly ministry. Nearly 2,000 years ago, on the last great day of the Feast of Tabernacles, during the ceremony known as "The Pouring Out of the Water" Jesus revealed Himself and took center stage.

Here's what took place during this solemn ceremony. A million or more people who had been dwelling in booths (tents) in Jerusalem arose early on the last day of the feast. The priests, Levites, singers, musicians, and temple guard gathered with excitement for this divinely inspired event. From the temple came forth the High Priest carrying the sacred golden vessel. Following him were the attendant priests, the worshipers, and the pomp and pageantry of the temple guard.

They walked from the temple slowly and majestically, down the Temple Mount as they sang from Isaiah 12:3: *"With joy shall ye draw water out of the wells of salvation."* They eventually made their way down the Temple Mount to the sacred stream of Siloam which flowed out of the earth under the Temple Mount. The types and shadows in this ceremony are amazing, especially when you consider who the temple really is. The High Priest would then dip the golden vessel into the clear water of the stream of Siloam, and with the filled vessel in his hand he would lead the procession back to the temple. The people would continue to sing from Isaiah 12:3-4: *"Behold, God is my salvation; I will trust, and not be afraid: for the Lord Jehovah is my strength and*

HANNAH ROARS

my song; he also is become my salvation. Therefore with joy shall ye draw water out of the wells of salvation." Then came the final, great ceremonial act. The High Priest would take the water in the golden vessel and pour it upon the altar while the people would shout: *"With joy shall ye draw water out of the wells of salvation!"*

It was at that very moment that Jesus stepped forth, taking His rightful place as the true High Priest, and lifted up His hands to the surprised multitudes on Mount Moriah and cried with a loud voice: *"If any man thirst, let him come unto me, and drink. He that believeth on me, as the Scripture hath said, out of his belly shall flow rivers of living water"* (John 7:37-38). What silence must have fallen upon the people! Who could be so bold and daring as to take the place of the High Priest and go even further by declaring Himself to be the fountain of living water springing up unto eternal life? The Jewish people had always believed that their Messiah would appear on this last great day of the feast, and many still do.

It is vitally important to note that it was at the Feast of Tabernacles that Jesus revealed Himself as the giver of the Holy Spirit, as rivers of living waters. Most Christians have associated the rivers of living water with the gift of the Holy Spirit received at the Feast of Pentecost. I would not want to devalue the wonderful measure of life and experience of the Holy Spirit we have received in our Pentecostal experience, but our Pentecostal experience has only been the earnest, the down payment, and guarantee of the fullness of the Spirit. As we previously discussed, the Feast of Tabernacles occurred at the time of the harvest; and Jesus said that the harvest is the end of the age. We have come to the hour when the rivers of life are going to flow more powerfully than we could ever have imagined. As I stated previously, I don't think we can exaggerate the coming move of the rivers of God in and through us. God is not a God of hype or false comfort, but a God of truth and reality.

Now unto him that is able to do exceeding abundantly above all that we ask or think, according to the power that worketh in us (Ephesians 3:20).

The above verse clearly states that God is about to supercede our prayer requests and our thought life (imagination). The roaring and

Roaring Rivers

thundering of these rivers will be undeniable. Look again at the glorious result of the rivers of life that will affect the whole earth.

And, behold, the glory of the God of Israel came from the way of the east: and his voice was like a noise of many waters: and the earth shined with his glory (Ezekiel 43:2).

Remember, it's the rivers of living water *in you* that release His glory in the earth.

Christ in you, the hope of glory (Colossians 1:27).

The Spotless Bride

The releasing of the rivers of life is so important to God that He speaks of it in the last chapter of the Bible. All good authors want to make the last chapter of their books climactically significant and forceful. And God, being the best author, has certainly done so with the last chapters in the book of Revelation. Revelation 21 speaks of that which is most important, significant, and beloved to God—His Bride, His Church.

Come hither, I will shew thee the bride, the Lamb's wife. And he carried me away in the spirit to a great and high mountain, and shewed me that great city, the holy Jerusalem, descending out of heaven from God, having the glory of God (Revelation 21:9–11).

The heavenly Jerusalem is actually symbolic language for the bride, His church. It would be laughable if it weren't so sad how many Christians get excited about a physical cubed city that would be 1,500 miles wide, 1,500 miles long, and yes, 1,500 miles high. It would literally descend upon the earth and flatten the Middle East, parts of northeastern Africa, parts of the Mediterranean Sea and parts of southeastern Europe. Even more astounding than the width of this city, if Revelation 21 were to be literally interpreted, is the fact that it would go well beyond Earth's atmosphere and into space. The Earth's stratosphere, which includes the ozone layer, is only about 30 miles high.

HANNAH ROARS

The Pearly Gates

It's time to tip over this sacred cow, if you haven't already. God is talking about His beloved bride, His church in the last chapters of His amazing book. You are the focus of God, and He included you in the final chapters of His book. The detailed descriptions of that city in Revelation 21 all have to do with qualities that He is building into His bride. For example, the twelve gates described as twelve pearls are character traits He is building into us. A pearl is formed when something slips into an oyster which acts as an irritant that causes the oyster to produce a beautiful, brilliant substance around the irritant. God has allowed many irritants (these can often be people) and hardships in the lives of His people. But don't get discouraged; He has placed them there to birth something beautiful, precious, and costly in you. The birth of a pearl is a truly miraculous event. Unlike gemstones, which must be mined from the earth and cut and polished to bring forth their beauty, pearls from oysters are born complete, with a shimmering iridescence and inner glow like no other gem on earth.

Revelation 21:12 tells us that these twelve pearly gates were each named after the twelve tribes of Israel. I would encourage you to look up the meaning of the names of each tribe. These names will help you discover more of the character traits and qualities God is building into His city, which is actually you and me, His bride.

But ye are come unto mount Sion, and unto the city of the living God, the heavenly Jerusalem, and to an innumerable company of angels, to the general assembly and church of the firstborn (Hebrews 12:22-23).

The Temple

Notice how He goes from talking about His city (the church which is His bride) in Revelation 21 to talking about His throne in Revelation 22. The place of His throne is obviously His temple, and it should be clear to every believer who the temple of God is throughout the book of Revelation; but because of strong delusion that has plagued many in the church, I will make it plain. You are God's temple. You are God's eternal house and habitation. The entire New Testament makes this

Roaring Rivers

undeniably clear. It seems from these last two chapters in the Bible that God has something passionately on His mind; that something is you, His church, His Bride. Oh that we would comprehend the depth of the passion and love that He has for us! A myriad of physical and emotional ills would be cured in the members of His body if we would just get a revelation of the depth and reality of His love.

> **May be able to comprehend with all saints what is the breadth, and length, and depth, and height; and to know the love of Christ, which passeth knowledge, that ye might be filled with all the fulness of God (Ephesians 3:18-19).**

Where Did the Temple Go?

You are the city so highly spoken of in Revelation 21, and you are the place of His throne mentioned in chapter 22 that has a river of life flowing out of it. This river of life will remove the curse from the earth. Remember the ceremony of the pouring out of the water that took place on the last great day of the Feast of Tabernacles. There was a stream, a river, flowing out from under the natural temple. There is a river of life in you, God's ultimate temple and final dwelling place. You are God's temple. You are God's house and habitation in the earth, and His Spirit (rivers of living water) will flow out of you to bring life to all of creation.

> **The creature** [creation] **itself also shall be delivered from the bondage of corruption into the glorious liberty of the children of God (Romans 8:21).**

God refers to His temple over a dozen times in the book of Revelation. But John the Revelator declares something I recently came to understand. In Revelation 21:22, John stated that he saw no temple in the city. How could this be when he writes about the temple in great detail many other times elsewhere in the book of Revelation?

> **And I saw no temple therein: for the Lord God Almighty and the Lamb are the temple of it (Revelation 21:22).**

Notice that John didn't state that there was no temple in the city, for that would contradict the many times that the temple is mentioned elsewhere in Revelation. He said he saw no temple therein, and goes on to emphasize that the Lord God Almighty and the Lamb are the temple. This is an amazing phenomenon that John describes. The temple is obviously there, because John refers to it many times, and chapter 22 speaks of the throne of God which has been and always will be in His temple. But the temple will not be the emphasis. The temple will not be the focus. God will be seen. He is the focus. *Our lives will be swallowed up in Him.* God will be *"all in all"* (1 Corinthians 15:28). The old creation man will not be seen anymore. It will be Christ in us, God's new creation, many-membered man in the earth. The time is upon us when the church (God's temple) will no longer be able to focus upon and even worship itself as it clearly has done throughout its history. The church will finally be the light of the world it is called to be and will point people to Him and not to itself. This will allow church life and the relationships between the members of His body to be more vital and fulfilling than ever. We will finally be that glorious church without spot or wrinkle. But it will not be the church's glory; it will be the glory of God. Speaking of the city, the bride, the church:

Having the glory of God [notice, it's God's glory]**...And the city had no need of the sun, neither of the moon, to shine in it: for the glory of God did lighten it, and the Lamb is the light thereof (Revelation 21:11, 23).**

No More Curse

Notice the results of this glorious river of life that flows out of His throne that is within His city, His church:

And there shall be no more curse (Revelation 22:3).

Creation will finally be delivered from the bondage of decay and corruption. What God is birthing through the intense groaning and travail of His Hannahs, His church, will be used to remove the curse. The groaning and travail of the Spirit for this hour is for much more than simply another revival or temporary awakening. Christ is going to be fully formed within us. The Jesus ministry will be seen in the earth

Roaring Rivers

again, only this time in a many-membered body that will completely transform all of creation.

My little children, of whom I travail in birth again until Christ be formed in you (Galatians 4:19).

We must know and understand the hope to which we have been called. Why is this important? Because there is a principle taught through Scripture that if you can see it, then it is yours to begin to walk in.

The secret things belong unto the Lord our God: but those things which are revealed belong unto us and to our children for ever, that we may do all the words of this law (Deuteronomy 29:29).

Go Ahead, Jump!

It's time to abandon ourselves in Him. That is the Hebrew meaning of the word *hallelujah*—to praise God with abandon. Praise and worship is not just something we do in a church service. It is how we live our daily lives. We must live our lives fully in Him and allow Him to live His life fully in us. This is the prayer that Jesus prayed in John 17, and it will be answered. How can we possibly want to live for anything else? This is true worship—living for Him, seeking Him, and knowing Him. Who will pay the price?

Chapter 9: Roaring 101

Chapter 9
Roaring 101

The ABCs of How to Roar

The secret to our future can be found in our daily routine. We must daily release the roar of God as Hannah did by praying the Word of God and releasing prophetic decrees. Because we are new covenant believers, we can do something that Hannah could not—we can take our prayer life to a whole new level by praying in the Holy Spirit. New Testament believers should follow the New Testament instructions on prayer. There are a number of places that instruct us to pray in the Spirit, but the definitive chapter on praying in the Spirit is found in 1 Corinthians 14. Paul talks about praying in the Spirit and praying with our understanding. Like Paul, we should not do just one or the other; we should do both.

In 1 Corinthians 14, Paul clearly uses the terms *"praying in tongues"* and *"praying in the Spirit"* interchangeably. Unlike many well-known Christian leaders today, Paul does not equate praying in the Spirit with simply praying inspirationally or exuberantly in one's known language. He clearly states that when you pray in the Spirit, you are *not* praying with your understanding. In other words, you do not understand what you are praying, because you are not praying in a language you understand; you are praying in an "unknown tongue." Paul even takes it a step further by stating that "no man" understands you when you are praying in tongues because you are not speaking unto men when you pray in tongues; you are speaking unto God.

> **For he that speaketh in an unknown tongue speaketh not unto men, but unto God: for no man understandeth him; howbeit in the spirit he speaketh mysteries (1 Corinthians 14:2).**

HANNAH ROARS

It is unfortunate that many today confuse Paul's teaching on *praying* in the Spirit or in tongues, discussed in 1 Corinthians 14, with his teaching on the *gift* of diverse kinds of tongues mentioned in 1 Corinthians 12:10. Praying in the Spirit involves speaking or praying out divine mysteries or secrets to God, while the gift of tongues involves speaking a word of edification or instruction to the church and is accompanied by the gift of interpretation of tongues, mentioned in 1 Corinthians 12.

Praying Divine Mysteries

Paul said in 1 Corinthians 14 that when you pray in the Spirit (in tongues), your spirit man is praying divine mysteries to God. God made man an intelligent being in His very own image, but none of us are intelligent enough to know exactly what we are to pray for and how we are to pray in every situation. However, our spirit man, who is directly joined to the Lord, can pray what our minds are not capable of knowing through the Holy Spirit.

> **But he that is joined unto the Lord is one spirit (1 Corinthians 6:17).**

> **Likewise the Spirit also helpeth our infirmities: for we know not what we should pray for as we ought: but the Spirit itself maketh intercession for us with groanings which cannot be uttered. And he that searcheth the hearts knoweth what is the mind of the Spirit, because he maketh intercession for the saints according to the will of God (Romans 8:26-27).**

What an amazing passage. We can learn to flow with the Holy Spirit in prayer and pray for things we would never otherwise have known to pray for. We can actually pray forth the perfect will of God for our lives and others.

Standing on the Shoulders of Giants

I learned the importance of praying in the Holy Spirit from men and women who have gone before us who learned how to follow the will and plan of God for their lives and accomplished great things on the earth for the Lord. Near the end of his life, the apostle Paul said that he

Roaring 101

"finished his course." In other words, he had finished and fulfilled the plan and purpose of God for his life. Would one in a hundred Christians who were about to meet the Lord be able to say the same? Paul had something in common with other great men and women who greatly impacted the earth for the glory of God. They fulfilled and finished their mission without getting derailed because they prayed in tongues often. In fact, Paul said, *"I thank my God, I speak with tongues more than ye all"* (1 Corinthians 14:18).

Divine Intervention

We should set time aside daily to not only pray and decree God's Word with our understanding, but to pray with the Spirit in our heavenly language. One night while I was praying in tongues for a considerable length of time, I tapped into a more fervent anointing and flow of the Spirit and sensed that I was praying for something rather urgent. I didn't know what I was praying about because I was not praying with my understanding, as Paul put it. But I felt it was important to know what I was praying about so I did what Paul instructed us to do in 1 Corinthians 14:13—I prayed that I may interpret what I had been praying in tongues. An interpretation is not a word-for-word translation, but is often more of a summary.

When I asked the Lord what I was praying about so fervently in the Spirit, the interpretation, or summary, bubbled up from my spirit man and registered on my mind. I knew instantly that I had been praying about a car accident that my wife was going to potentially be involved in, but that my prayers in the Spirit had released divine intervention. I went to bed knowing all was well. My wife had already been asleep for some time and I did not feel the need to wake her because I knew in my spirit that it was already *prayed through* and taken care of, and that I had the victory. The next day when my wife got home from work, she said to me, "You won't believe what happened to me today."

Before she could go on to explain, I interrupted her and said, "Let me guess—you came very close to being in a car accident, but you were miraculously delivered."

HANNAH ROARS

She said, "That's right. How did you know?" So I told her of my experience while praying in tongues the night before. She went on to explain that a large truck was heading right toward her and there was no time and nothing she could do to avoid the collision, but that something moved her car sideways, completely out of harm's way, right before the impact. We knew that Holy Spirit-empowered prayer had released intervention. That is one of many times where Holy Spirit-empowered prayer has birthed miraculous, heavenly intervention in our lives.

I can tell you of many unnecessary hardships and mistakes that I avoided by taking time to pray in the Holy Spirit. I can also tell you of many unnecessary hardships and mistakes that I did not avoid because of spiritual laziness and not taking the time to pray in the Holy Ghost as I should.

Lord of the Breakthrough

When David was finally anointed to be king over all of Israel, the Philistines, the enemies of God's people, heard of it and wanted to put a stop to David's rulership.

The Philistines also came and spread themselves in the valley of Rephaim (2 Samuel 5:18).

Rephaim means "giant."[17] Have you ever been in a valley of giants? David had waited for nearly thirteen years for the fulfillment of his kingly prophecy, enduring manifold tests and trials. Now the day of fulfillment had finally come, but the enemy was there to try to stop it. Don't think for an instant that the enemy will not try to stop you from walking in your kingly anointing. David did not rely on his own strength but did what he knew to do and what he would become known for during most of his reign—David inquired of the Lord. The Lord told him to go up against the Philistines and that He would certainly deliver them into David's hands. That's when David approached the battle and got a revelation of God as the *Lord of the breakthrough*. God was about to turn the valley of giants into a place of tremendous breakthrough!

---

17. Strong, *Strong's Exhaustive Concordance*, H7497.

Roaring 101

And David came to Baalperazim, and David smote them there, and said, The Lord hath broken forth upon mine enemies before me, as the breach [breaking forth] **of waters. Therefore he called the name of that place Baalperazim (2 Samuel 5:20).**

Baalperazim literally means, *"the Lord of breaking forth."*[18] The image is of flooding waters breaking through a dam. Remember, Jesus said in John 7 that waters would be released in His people. If we want to experience the breaking forth of the waters of the Lord that will bring the breakthrough in our lives and in the earth, then we must cooperate with Him in the release of those waters. God will release the waters of breakthrough out of those who learn the secret of letting the rivers of living water flow out of them.

Let's Go Deeper

Praying in the Spirit involves more than just sputtering forth a few words in tongues. We must learn how to pray in the Spirit with an anointing. Just as we have all experienced preaching with and without an anointing, so it is with praying in the Spirit. If you will start praying in the Spirit every day for extended periods of time, you will learn how to quickly enter the deeper realms of prayer and flow with the anointing of the Holy Spirit. At first, it might seem like it's almost a labor to pray in the Spirit, but after a while you will hit a gusher, so to speak, and begin to pray with the anointing. Your heavenly prayer language will roll out of you freely. That's when the breakthrough comes. That's when victory comes and His power is released to perform His will in the earth.

Have it be your goal to learn to get to the place where tongues begin to flow out of you with a strong Holy Spirit unction or anointing. You might start out plowing, so to speak, but continue on until you learn to pray under a powerful anointing of the Holy Spirit. It is a matter of learning how to yield to Him and flow with Him, praying His perfect will. It's a lot like a skilled surfer who learns how to discover and ride out the ocean waves. Like any truly valuable skill, this will take time, commitment, dedication, and persistence. The Holy Spirit isn't going

---

18. Strong, *Strong's Exhaustive Concordance.*, H1188.

to come upon you and flow through you without your permission and cooperation. But as you seek Him, yield to Him, and give Him permission to flow and roar through you, you will enter into that deeper realm of prayer. Tongues will begin to flow out of you with greater power and stronger anointing. That's when His roar and thunder will be released. His power will be greatly unleashed to accomplish His purposes in the earth.

When you enter into a strong prayer flow and anointing, continue to pray as forcefully and as fast as you can. I learned this truth from great men and women of God, from God's generals of the past who have been used mightily of God in the advancement of His kingdom. I read where one of God's generals explained that when he would enter into that stronger anointing to pray, he would pray in tongues as hard and as fast as he could. He would continue to pray that way until he sensed a release or a note of victory in his spirit. Praying like this will always birth miracles and salvations, resulting in the advancement of God's kingdom.

Who hath heard such a thing? who hath seen such things? Shall the earth be made to bring forth in one day? or shall a nation be born at once? for as soon as Zion travailed, she brought forth her children (Isaiah 66:8).

Who Will Rise Up?

There are relatively few Christians today who are capable of entering into this deeper realm of praying in the Holy Spirit with an anointing. God is calling many more to join with Him in entering into this type of walk so that His roar can be released in the earth. Because of the urgency of the hour and the final harvest that is upon us, He must have more Hannahs. He must have those who know how to pray in that deeper realm and release His glorious rivers that will cover the earth. The time is short. God is calling us to say *no* to the flesh and all other distractions and spend time birthing and praying forth His divine purposes. He needs us, His body, His bride, to birth His purposes in the earth. I have heard many leaders in the church state that God in His sovereignty can do whatever He wants, independently of us. This is totally contrary to New

Roaring 101

Testament doctrine which clearly reveals that God, in His sovereignty, has covenanted Himself to His church to accomplish His purposes. Jesus is the Head and we are His body. It states in 1 Corinthians 12:21 that the head cannot say to the foot, *"I have no need of you."*

For we are labourers together with God (1 Corinthians 3:9).

Resolution Precedes Revolution

The flesh, the mind, and the devil will fight us when it comes to entering the deeper realms of anointed prayer. But Christ has given us authority to walk in total victory. The Scriptures clearly teach that we have the ability, because of Calvary, to present our bodies to God as living sacrifices, renew our minds with the Word of God, resist the devil, and enforce God's defeat over him.

It is important to understand that in the spirit realm, there is no time or distance. So as you learn to pray in the Holy Spirit and flow with the Holy Spirit, you will enter into the realm where the possibilities of what God can do in and through you are limitless. Your prayers will be limited to His will only. Why would anyone want anything outside of the will of God anyway?

We must present our bodies to God and renew our minds as the Scripture commands. The Lord and the things of the Spirit will become more real to us than the physical world. Then, we will be able to bring the realities of the heavenly realm into the physical world. *God's will will be done on earth as it is in heaven.* It's time to move on from *"glory to glory"* and seek God as never before. By doing this, we can be used of Him through prayer, intercession, and travail to birth this move of God in the earth that He so desires. We can sense the urgency of it. God wants to release His roar and His thunder through us. His voice will be heard once again as it was in Genesis 1, at the creation. This time, His voice will be heard and His purposes will be accomplished through His body, His new creation man in the earth. Be determined to respond to His call and fulfill all that He has purposed for you to do in this climactic hour.

Don't grow weary as you watch those in the world appear to be in a state of ease and productivity while you appear to be in a state

HANNAH ROARS

of barrenness and endless adversity. You were not chosen by accident to live in these days of great shaking, adversity, and hardship. It's time to get your eyes off of others and even off of your own current circumstances. It's time to look at God's amazing, covenant promises for those who live at this time. It's time to look to the Lord and take the limits off Him. Everything is about to change. It's already begun.

God, in His divine wisdom and foresight, has allowed and perhaps even orchestrated your present situation of barrenness and adversity so that you will rise up and press into His presence and become the overcomer you are called to be. God's calling is indeed a high one. We are heirs of God and joint-heirs with Christ (see Romans 8:17). The Lord has called you to be His eternal companion and partner. He desires that you become so close and united with Him that He is able to produce something truly extraordinary in and through you. God is birthing something new, glorious, and unprecedented in the earth. It's time to roar!

Appendix

In addition to praying in the Spirit, it is important to pray and decree His Word. Here is the list of Scriptures I mentioned in the book that I believe the Lord would have His body release for this hour.

General Scriptures on the Power of Prayer

> Put me in remembrance: let us plead together: declare thou, that thou mayest be justified (Isaiah 43:26).

> And this is the confidence that we have in him, that, if we ask any thing according to his will, he heareth us: and if we know that he hear us, whatsoever we ask, we know that we have the petitions that we desired of him (1 John 5:14-15).

> The earth is the Lord's, and the fulness thereof; the world, and they that dwell therein (Psalm 24:1).

> Thy kingdom come, thy will be done in earth, as it is in heaven (Matthew 6:10).

> The effectual fervent prayer of a righteous man availeth much (James 5:16).

Scriptural Things to Pray For

1. Pray for an outpouring of God's Spirit.

> Ask ye of the Lord rain in the time of the latter rain; so the Lord shall make bright clouds, and give them showers of rain, to every one grass in the field (Zechariah 10:1).

HANNAH ROARS

2. Pray for boldness and for the demonstration of God's power.

> **And now, Lord, behold their threatenings: and grant unto thy servants, that with all boldness they may speak thy word, by stretching forth thine hand to heal; and that signs and wonders may be done by the name of thy holy child Jesus (Acts 4:29-30).**

3. And pray for laborers!

> **Pray ye therefore the Lord of the harvest, that he will send forth labourers into his harvest. (Matthew 9:38).**

4. Take authority over the powers of darkness, forbidding their operation.

> **Verily I say unto you, Whatsoever ye shall bind on earth shall be bound in heaven: and whatsoever ye shall loose on earth shall be loosed in heaven. Again I say unto you, That if two of you shall agree on earth as touching any thing that they shall ask, it shall be done for them of my Father which is in heaven (Matthew 18:18-19).**

> **In whom the god of this world hath blinded the minds of them which believe not, lest the light of the glorious gospel of Christ, who is the image of God, should shine unto them (2 Corinthians 4:4).**

5. Pray that God would turn the hearts of leaders toward righteousness and that godly people would come into places of authority.

> **I exhort therefore, that, first of all, supplications, prayers, intercessions, and giving of thanks, be made for all men; for kings, and for all that are in authority; that we may lead a quiet and peaceable life in all godliness and honesty. For this is good and acceptable in the sight of God our Saviour; who will have all men to be saved, and to come unto the knowledge of the truth (1 Timothy 2:1–4).**

> **When the righteous are in authority, the people rejoice: but when the wicked beareth rule, the people mourn (Proverbs 29:2).**

Appendix

> The king's heart is in the hand of the Lord, as the rivers of water: he turneth it whithersoever he will (Proverbs 21:1).

6. Pray for the free spreading of the gospel and for God's children around the world to be delivered from wicked men.

    > Finally, brethren, pray for us, that the word of the Lord may have free course, and be glorified, even as it is with you: and that we may be delivered from unreasonable and wicked men: for all men have not faith (2 Thessalonians 3:1-2).

    > Let the priests, the ministers of the Lord, weep between the porch and the altar, and let them say, Spare thy people, O Lord, and give not thine heritage to reproach, that the heathen should rule over them: wherefore should they say among the people, Where is their God? (Joel 2:17).

    > Thus saith the Lord God; Remove the diadem, and take off the crown: this shall not be the same: exalt him that is low, and abase him that is high. I will overturn, overturn, overturn, it: and it shall be no more, until he come whose right it is; and I will give it him (Ezekiel 21:26-27).

    > That the blood of all the prophets, which was shed from the foundation of the world, may be required of this generation; from the blood of Abel unto the blood of Zacharias, which perished between the altar and the temple: verily I say unto you, It shall be required of this generation (Luke 11:50-51).

    > And in her was found the blood of prophets, and of saints, and of all that were slain upon the earth (Revelation 18:24).

    > For the day of vengeance is in mine heart, and the year of my redeemed is come (Isaiah 63:4).

    > The day of vengeance of our God (Isaiah 61:2).

7. Pray these Holy Spirit-inspired prayers for the body of Christ. It's time for a great awakening.

HANNAH ROARS

Cease not to give thanks for you, making mention of you in my prayers; that the God of our Lord Jesus Christ, the Father of glory, may give unto you the spirit of wisdom and revelation in the knowledge of him: the eyes of your understanding being enlightened; that ye may know what is the hope of his calling, and what the riches of the glory of his inheritance in the saints, and what is the exceeding greatness of his power to us-ward who believe, according to the working of his mighty power, which he wrought in Christ, when he raised him from the dead, and set him at his own right hand in the heavenly places, far above all principality, and power, and might, and dominion, and every name that is named, not only in this world, but also in that which is to come: and hath put all things under his feet, and gave him to be the head over all things to the church, which is his body, the fulness of him that filleth all in all (Ephesians 1:16–23).

For this cause I bow my knees unto the Father of our Lord Jesus Christ...That he would grant you, according to the riches of his glory, to be strengthened with might by his Spirit in the inner man; that Christ may dwell in your hearts by faith; that ye, being rooted and grounded in love, may be able to comprehend with all saints what is the breadth, and length, and depth, and height; and to know the love of Christ, which passeth knowledge, that ye might be filled with all the fulness of God. Now unto him that is able to do exceeding abundantly above all that we ask or think, according to the power that worketh in us, unto him be glory in the church by Christ Jesus throughout all ages, world without end. Amen (Ephesians 3:14,16–21).

My little children, of whom I travail in birth again until Christ be formed in you (Galatians 4:19).

Prophetic Prayers and Decrees for This Hour

Be silent, O all flesh, before the Lord: for he is raised up out of his holy habitation (Zechariah 2:13).

Appendix

Come, my people, enter thou into thy chambers, and shut thy doors about thee: hide thyself as it were for a little moment, until the indignation be overpast. For, behold, the Lord cometh out of his place to punish the inhabitants of the earth for their iniquity: the earth also shall disclose her blood, and shall no more cover her slain (Isaiah 26:20-21).

The Lord shall go forth as a mighty man, he shall stir up jealousy like a man of war: he shall cry, yea, roar; he shall prevail against his enemies. I have long time holden my peace; I have been still, and refrained myself: now will I cry like a travailing woman; I will destroy and devour at once. I will make waste mountains and hills, and dry up all their herbs; and I will make the rivers islands, and I will dry up the pools (Isaiah 42:13–15).

For he put on righteousness as a breastplate, and an helmet of salvation upon his head; and he put on the garments of vengeance for clothing, and was clad with zeal as a cloak. According to their deeds, accordingly he will repay, fury to his adversaries, recompence to his enemies; to the islands he will repay recompence. So shall they fear the name of the Lord from the west, and his glory from the rising of the sun. When the enemy shall come in like a flood, the Spirit of the Lord shall lift up a standard against him (Isaiah 59:17–19).

Therefore wait ye upon me, saith the Lord, until the day that I rise up to the prey: for my determination is to gather the nations, that I may assemble the kingdoms, to pour upon them mine indignation, even all my fierce anger: for all the earth shall be devoured with the fire of my jealousy (Zephaniah 3:8).

Then the Lord awaked as one out of sleep, and like a mighty man that shouteth by reason of wine. And he smote his enemies in the hinder parts: he put them to a perpetual reproach (Psalm 78:65-66).

HANNAH ROARS

The Son of man shall send forth his angels, and they shall gather out of his kingdom all things that offend, and them which do iniquity (Matthew 13:41).

Thus saith the Lord God; Behold, I am against the shepherds; and I will require my flock at their hand, and cause them to cease from feeding the flock; neither shall the shepherds feed themselves any more; for I will deliver my flock from their mouth, that they may not be meat for them (Ezekiel 34:10).

Why do the heathen rage, and the people imagine a vain thing? The kings of the earth set themselves, and the rulers take counsel together, against the Lord, and against his anointed, saying, Let us break their bands asunder, and cast away their cords from us. He that sitteth in the heavens shall laugh: the Lord shall have them in derision. Then shall he speak unto them in his wrath, and vex them in his sore displeasure. ...Ask of me, and I shall give thee the heathen for thine inheritance, and the uttermost parts of the earth for thy possession. Thou shalt break them with a rod of iron; thou shalt dash them in pieces like a potter's vessel (Psalm 2:1–5, 8-9).

And I will overthrow the throne of kingdoms, and I will destroy the strength of the kingdoms of the heathen; and I will overthrow the chariots, and those that ride in them; and the horses and their riders shall come down, every one by the sword of his brother. In that day, saith the Lord of hosts, will I take thee, O Zerubbabel, my servant, the son of Shealtiel, saith the Lord, and will make thee as a signet: for I have chosen thee, saith the Lord of hosts (Haggai 2:22-23).

Thine hand shall find out all thine enemies: thy right hand shall find out those that hate thee. Thou shalt make them as a fiery oven in the time of thine anger: the Lord shall swallow them up in his wrath, and the fire shall devour them. Their fruit shalt thou destroy from the earth, and their seed from among the children of men (Psalm 21:8–10).

Appendix

Thou, even thou, art to be feared: and who may stand in thy sight when once thou art angry? Thou didst cause judgment to be heard from heaven; the earth feared, and was still, when God arose to judgment, to save all the meek of the earth. Selah (Psalm 76:7–9).

Christ hath redeemed us from the curse of the law, being made a curse for us: for it is written, Cursed is every one that hangeth on a tree: that the blessing of Abraham might come on the Gentiles through Jesus Christ; that we might receive the promise of the Spirit through faith (Galatians 3:13-14).

And the Lord shall make thee the head, and not the tail; and thou shalt be above only, and thou shalt not be beneath (Deuteronomy 28:13).

Who satisfieth thy mouth with good things; so that thy youth is renewed like the eagle's. The Lord executeth righteousness and judgment for all that are oppressed (Psalm 103:5-6).

Be glad then, ye children of Zion, and rejoice in the Lord your God: for he hath given you the former rain moderately, and he will cause to come down for you the rain, the former rain, and the latter rain in the first month. And the floors shall be full of wheat, and the vats shall overflow with wine and oil. And I will restore to you the years that the locust hath eaten, the cankerworm, and the caterpiller, and the palmerworm, my great army which I sent among you. And ye shall eat in plenty, and be satisfied, and praise the name of the Lord your God, that hath dealt wondrously with you: and my people shall never be ashamed (Joel 2:23–26).

It shall come to pass in the last days, that the mountain of the Lord's house shall be established in the top of the mountains, and shall be exalted above the hills; and all nations shall flow unto it. And many people shall go and say, Come ye, and let us go up to the mountain of the Lord, to the house of the God of Jacob; and he will teach us of his ways, and we will walk in his paths: for out of Zion shall go forth the law, and the word of the Lord from Jerusalem. And he shall judge among the nations, and shall rebuke many people: and they shall beat their swords into plowshares, and their spears into pruninghooks: nation shall not lift up sword against nation, neither shall they learn war any more (Isaiah 2:2–4; see also Micah 4:1–3).

For there is nothing covered, that shall not be revealed; neither hid, that shall not be known. Therefore whatsoever ye have spoken in darkness shall be heard in the light; and that which ye have spoken in the ear in closets shall be proclaimed upon the housetops (Luke 12:2-3).

Call unto me, and I will answer thee, and shew thee great and mighty things, which thou knowest not (Jeremiah 33:3).

Howbeit when he, the Spirit of truth, is come, he will guide you into all truth: for he shall not speak of Himself; but whatsoever he shall hear, that shall he speak: and he will shew you things to come (John 16:13).

About the Author

Greg Buzzanco is the founder and pastor of Triumphant Life Church in Erie, Pennsylvania. The ministry also includes Triumphant Life Christian Academy (K-12), a Bible training center, and Triumphant Life Church in Jamestown, New York. Greg has traveled the world speaking in churches and conferences and currently lives in Erie, Pennsylvania with his wife, Susan, and their two sons.

Find out more about Greg Buzzanco and Triumphant Life Church at www.triumphantlifechurch.com.

www.ingramcontent.com/pod-product-compliance
Lightning Source LLC
Chambersburg PA
CBHW071737080526
44588CB00013B/2067